JOURNAL OF THE TRAIL

Compiled and Edited
by
Stewart E. Glazier
and
Robert S. Clark

Design and Maps by
Smart Design, Inc., Salt Lake City

The Mormon Pioneer Trail is "a trail of tragedy, a trail of faith, a trail of devotion, a trail of consecration, even the consecration of life itself...." Terrible was the suffering of those who came here [to Martin's Cove] to find some protection from the heavy storms of that early winter. With their people hungry, cold and dying from sheer exhaustion, they came up into this cove for shelter. And then they died here, some 56 people. They are buried somewhere in this earth. We stand here with bare heads and grateful hearts for their sacrifices, and the sacrifices of all who were with them along this tragic trail.... [May this site be visited by] generations yet to come, who, like we, may bow their heads in reverent remembrance of our forebears who paid so costly a price for the faith which they carried in their hearts.

--President Gordon B. Hinckley,
Church News, August 22, 1992.

President Harold B. Lee told me once that inspiration comes easier when you can set foot on the site related to the need for it.

--President Boyd K. Packer,
Brigham Young Magazine,
November 1995, p. 47.

The Spirit has confirmed to me the important responsibility we have to see that the legacy of faith of our pioneer forefathers is never lost. We can derive great strength, particularly our youth, from understanding our church history.

--Elder M. Russell Ballard,
Ensign, November 1995, p.6.

JOURNAL OF THE TRAIL

INDEX

CASPER TO SOUTH PASS

APPROX. 150 MILES

Casper
Red Buttes
Prospect Hill
Willow Springs
North Platte River
Horse Creek (Greasewood Creek)
Independence Rock
Devil's Gate
Martin's Cove
Split Rock
Cottonwood Creek
Three Crossings
Ice Slough
Sixth Crossing
Rocky Ridge
Willie Memorial at Rock Creek
Strawberry Creek
Sweetwater River
Rock Creek
Willow Creek
Burnt Ranch
South Pass
Pacific Springs

INTRODUCTION

A reverence for sacred things gives context to all of life's experiences. That context is especially important when we learn about distant places and people who lived long ago. With the assistance of the Spirit, events that took place along the Mormon Trail can touch our hearts and inspire us to greater commitment. As President Boyd K. Packer has encouraged, our objective should be to "see the hand of the Lord in every hour and every moment of the Church from its beginning till now." The journals kept by the pioneers seem to cry out for us to see the hand of the Lord in the events described there. Without the Spirit, one may see the Mormon Trail as merely sagebrush and dusty paths. But a sensitive heart will discern the eloquent witness of what transpired there. When we begin to feel a spiritual kinship with those who walked these trails, our lives are strengthened and enriched.

The Mormon Trail is a sacred place, made holy by the sacrifice of the Lord's people. The story begins, of course, long before the first pioneers set foot on the Midwestern plains. It starts in 1820 in a grove of trees just outside Palmyra, New York. A young man knelt in prayer seeking direction from God, and received a glorious vision of our Heavenly Father and Jesus Christ. After receiving divine priesthood authority, the prophet Joseph Smith organized The Church of Jesus Christ of Latter-Day Saints on April 6, 1830.

The Kingdom of God grew rapidly, but faced constant persecution. The Saints moved to Kirtland, Ohio in 1831, where they built a temple and received all the keys of the priesthood necessary for the Lord's Kingdom. Next they established homes in Missouri, where the church continued to grow and receive additional revelations. When driven from

Missouri, the Saints in 1839 settled Nauvoo, Illinois, where they built a beautiful city and another temple. Unfortunately, persecution followed wherever they went. The enemies of the Church rejoiced when the Prophet Joseph Smith was martyred in Carthage, Illinois, on June 27, 1844. Before his death, however, the Prophet knew the Saints would move west. In 1842 he prophesied that the Saints would continue to suffer much affliction and "some of you will live to go and assist in making settlements and build cities and see the Saints become a mighty people in the midst of the Rocky Mountains."[1]

The Latter-Day Saints were not the only Americans looking west. The United States bought much of what is now the western states from France in 1803 with the Louisiana Purchase. That same year, a band of explorers led by Lewis and Clark traveled the entire breadth of the continent, eventually making their way to the Pacific Ocean. By the 1820's trappers, miners, and others started to push westward, looking for wealth from land, gold, and furs. By 1841, Oregon was recognized as a territory with great potential, and groups began to cross the plains along what became the Oregon Trail. Americans during that time believed it was the "Manifest Destiny" of the United States to own the entire western part of the continent, to control the land from the Atlantic Ocean to the Pacific.

After Joseph Smith's death in 1844, under the direction of the Quorum of the Twelve Apostles, the Saints hurried to complete the temple as they also prepared to leave Nauvoo. At the October General Conference in 1845, the Twelve encouraged the people to prepare for an orderly move from Nauvoo. The Saints were counseled to sell their property

---

[1] History of the Church, 5:85.

and prepare for an "exodus... to a far distant region of the west, where bigotry, intolerance and insatiable oppression lose their power."[2]

Unfortunately, the mobs would not allow them time to move in an organized fashion, and they were forced to begin to leave in the winter of 1846. Brigham Young and several others remained in Nauvoo to the last moment performing temple ordinances. The blessings of the temple were a source of strength to many who crossed the plains. One example among several is the account written by Sarah Rich, who labored with her husband in the Nauvoo Temple from 7:00 a.m. until midnight each day for several weeks: "Many were the blessings we had received in the house of the Lord, which has caused us joy and comfort in the midst of all our sorrows and enabled us to have faith in God, knowing he would guide us and sustain us in the unknown journey that lay before us. For if it had not been for the faith and knowledge that was bestowed upon us in that temple by the influence and help of the Spirit of the Lord, our journey would have been like one taking a leap in the dark."[3]

The main group of Saints leaving Nauvoo that winter moved about 300 miles across Iowa in 1846, camping at various places along the way. That summer, 541 men responded to assist the United States Army in the War with Mexico as the Mormon Battalion. The Saints eventually stopped in the fall of 1846 at Winter Quarters in western Iowa. They were more than 1,000 miles from the Great Salt Lake Valley.

---

[2] History of the Church, 7:478-80.

[3] Autobiography of Sarah DeArmon Pea Rich, as quoted in T. Madsen, Joseph the Prophet, p. 99.

Beginning in 1847 with the first "Pioneer Company", the exodus to the Great Salt Lake valley started. They still had to cross all of modern-day Nebraska and Wyoming, as well as eastern Utah. They followed parts of the existing Oregon Trail but in many places made their own trail across the plains. Sometimes the Mormon Trail went parallel to the Oregon Trail on the opposite side of a river, to keep the Saints separated from the more numerous groups headed for Oregon or California. (More than four times as many non-Mormons as Mormons crossed the plains during the mid-1800's.)

The first Pioneer Company consisted of 143 men, 3 women, and 2 children, who left Winter Quarters on April 5, 1847. They used all of the maps and resources available to them, and followed existing roads wherever possible. William Clayton was appointed camp historian and kept accurate records of mileage and key information that would help those who followed. In 1848 his work was published as the "Emigrant's Guide" and was one of the best resources available to both members and nonmembers alike for several years.

The "Laws or Rules" of the Pioneer Company as established on April 18, 1847, included the following:
1) The horn or bugle shall be blown every morning at 5 a.m., when every man is expected to arise and pray; then attend to his team, get breakfast and have everything finished so that the camp may start by 7 o'clock.
2) Each extra man is to travel on the off side of the team with his gun on his shoulder, loaded, and each driver have his gun so placed that he can lay hold of it at a moment's warning....
3) The brethren will halt for an hour about noon, and they must have their dinner ready cooked so as not to detain the camp for cooking.

4) When the camp halts for the night, wagons are to be drawn in a circle, and the horses to be all secured inside the circle when necessary.

5) The horn will blow at 8:30 p.m., when every man must return to his wagon and pray, except the night guard, and be in bed by 9 o'clock, at which time all fires must be put out.

6) The camp is to travel in close order, and no man to leave the camp 20 rods.[4]

7) Every man is to put as much interest in taking care of his brother's cattle, in preserving them, as he would his own, and no man will be indulged in idleness.

8) Every man is to have his gun and pistol in perfect order.

9) Let all start and keep together, and let the cannon bring up the rear, and the company guard to attend it, traveling along with the gun, and see that nothing is left behind at each stopping place.[5]

A couple of other "rules" used with other or later companies are also of interest:

"Resolved, that if any person while guard at night shall neglect his duty by sleep or otherwise, for the first offense he shall be reported publicly, and if afterwards found guilty of neglect he shall again be reported and be subjected to extra duty in the day time herding cattle.

"Resolved, that any member of this camp who shall indulge in profane language shall be reported to his captain of ten, and if he shall afterwards persist in profanity he shall be punished publicly."[6]

---

[4] One rod is equal to 16.5 feet; twenty rods is 330 feet.

[5] Howard Egan Diary, Pioneering the West, 1846-47, pp. 23-24.

[6] Little, From Kirtland to Salt Lake City, pp. 240-41.

Like the Oregon Trail, the Mormon Pioneer Trail generally followed the Platte River across Nebraska and eastern Wyoming. In central Wyoming, the trail cuts south to the Sweetwater River, and follows that river almost to the Continental Divide at South Pass. The trail then goes southeast past Fort Bridger and the Green River, through the difficult mountain passes east of the Great Salt Lake Valley, and into the valley through Emigration Canyon.

Although some of the 1847 Pioneer Company entered the valley beginning on July 22, Brigham Young and the last of the group didn't arrive until the 24th of July, which is the day now set aside to honor the Pioneers. While the group set to work immediately planting, cultivating, and irrigating, the hardships would continue for years to come. About 2,000 people came to Utah that first year, and several thousand more came each year for over twenty years. Saints wishing to gather to Zion were divided into "companies" of a few hundred people who would travel together along the trail, and generally were identified by the name of the captain called to lead the group.

By 1856, about 40,000 Church members had emigrated to Utah. Many were new converts from Europe who came to America by ship, boarded trains on the east coast, and eventually made it to one of the trailheads in the midwest where they would walk across the plains. Beginning in 1856 and continuing through 1860, many Saints pulled handcarts instead of having their belongings carried by wagons. The handcarts were much less expensive and could go faster than wagons. Except for two handcart companies in 1856, all the handcart companies made their way to Utah in good condition and without serious problems. By the time the transcontinental railroad was completed in 1869 approximately 70,000 Saints had crossed the plains in wagons or handcarts. By comparison, over 300,000 people had traveled the Oregon Trail to Oregon or California.

Handcart companies traveled light. The wooden handcarts were about four feet wide and six or seven feet long, with the "box" portion only three or four feet long and eight inches high. The carts themselves weighed approximately sixty pounds. (Both the weight and dimensions were smaller than many handcarts used by modern youth groups.) Sometimes, but not always, the carts had a canvas cover. Each cart would usually carry 400 or 500 pounds, which included flour, bedding, extra clothing, cooking utensils, and a tent. About five people were assigned to a handcart, and about twenty people shared a tent. Each person was allowed seventeen pounds of baggage, which included bedding, extra clothing, and cooking utensils. A member of the first handcart company of 1856, Mary Ann Jones, wrote: "Some wanted to take more than the allotted portion and put on extra clothes; thus many who were real thin became suddenly stout and as soon as the weighing was over, put their extra clothes back on the handcarts. But that did not last long. In a few days we had to have all weighed again and many were found with much more weight on the carts than allowed. One old sister carried a teapot and colander on her apron string all the way to Salt Lake. Another carried a hat box full of things, but she died on the way."[7]

Unfortunately, the Willie and Martin Companies, the last two of the five handcart companies of 1856, got a late start from Iowa City and encountered an early and extreme winter. In addition, the Hunt and Hodgett wagon companies, who were following behind the handcart companies, also faced the same

---

[7] As quoted in Hafen, Handcarts to Zion, p. 59.

overwhelming sacrifices. The sufferings and faith of these companies are beyond description. As word of their plight reached Salt Lake City, Brigham Young immediately sent out rescue parties, whose heroism literally saved hundreds of lives. Of the 404 members of the Willie Company, about 77 died along the way, including 15 who were buried at Rock Creek. The Martin Company started with 576, and lost about 145, many of whom were buried at Martin's Cove.

The journals in this book are organized primarily according to the location where events occurred. Although they are chronological within each section, the overall organization is in many places not chronological. The dates included in each entry heading are based on the chronology believed to be most accurate when all the records are taken together. In many instances, the dates are not actually part of the journal entries themselves, but are added here to aid understanding. The journals include descriptions of the first 1847 Pioneer Company, and records of the 1856 Willie, Martin, Hunt and Hodgett companies. Events from some of the rescue parties are also included. The journals selected here are only a small portion of the pioneer journals that have been kept. Further research and reading will add greatly to one's understanding of the events that transpired along the Mormon Trail. Although some of the accounts may be more accurately referred to as recollections or family histories than contemporaneous journals, for simplicity they are often referred to as journals without distinguishing among the types of records included. Spelling and word usage have sometimes been modified to aid understanding, but original spelling and usage have been maintained in many instances. The effort has not been one focused on technical scholarship, but rather has been an attempt to gather together materials that tell a true story in a powerful and spiritual way. As an additional effort to aid understanding, each chapter includes a brief description of the geography of the trail and surrounding areas.

To assist in understanding the Journals, it may be useful to picture the various groups and their locations at a particular point in time, such as mid-October, 1856. By that time, the first three handcart companies of 1856 had already reached Salt Lake City. The Utah Saints knew that the others were in trouble and had sent rescue parties with wagons and supplies, headed east. On October 15, the First Rescue Party was beyond Fort Bridger and the Green River and made camp on the Big Sandy River in eastern Wyoming. At the same time, the Willie Company was in central Wyoming and didn't know help was on its way. They were, however, further west than the other remaining companies, having reached Independence Rock and the Sweetwater River. The Martin and Hodgett Companies were further east, still traveling along the Platte River, not yet to Casper, Wyoming. The Hunt Company was close behind the other two. From that time, the Rescue Parties continued east and the others continued west until they made contact. Of course, the Willie Company was the first to receive assistance, meeting the first rescue party on October 21, and eventually reaching Salt Lake City on November 9 with the help of the wagons and food brought to them. The Martin, Hodgett, and Hunt Companies were not reached by any of the rescuers until October 28, and on November 9 the remaining rescue parties and the Martin, Hunt, and Hodgett Companies were still at Martin's Cove near Devil's Gate trying to get shelter from the horrible cold and prepare themselves for the remainder of the trek. The Martin Company arrived in Salt Lake City on November 30, with the last of the wagon companies arriving on December 15, 1856.

President Gordon B. Hinckley has said: "It is good to look to the past to gain appreciation for the present and perspective for the future. It is good to look upon the virtues of those who have gone before, to gain strength for whatever lies ahead. It is good to reflect upon the work of those who labored so hard and gained so little in this world, but out of whose dreams and early plans, so well nurtured, has come a great harvest of which we are the beneficiaries. Their tremendous example can become a compelling motivation for us all, for each of us is a pioneer in his own life, often in his own family, and many of us pioneer daily in trying to establish a gospel foothold in distant parts of the world."[8]

---

[8] Ensign, July 1984, p.3.

CHAPTER 1
THE TRAIL TO INDEPENDENCE ROCK

After leaving Nauvoo in 1846, the Saints traveled across Iowa before stopping at Winter Quarters on the border next to present day Omaha, Nebraska. When the Pioneer Company left Winter Quarters in the spring of 1847, they followed the **Platte River** across Nebraska, and continued along the **North Platte River** into central Wyoming. They passed **Fort Laramie**, which was located on the North Platte, and then came to present-day Casper, Wyoming, where they left the North Platte and headed southwest, toward **Independence Rock**. From Independence Rock they would begin following the **Sweetwater River** until the trail approached **South Pass**. (Most of the later pioneer companies also followed this route, although by 1856 the companies would be outfitted at Iowa City, Iowa, and pull their handcarts to Florence, Nebraska, where they intended to replenish their provisions. From there they generally followed the same trail as the earlier pioneers through Nebraska and Wyoming, and into Utah.)

Near Casper, the trail reached what is often referred to as the **Last Crossing of the Platte**. From here emigrants could either leave the North Platte and follow a trail that went due west, through **Emigrant Gap** (as did the 1847 Pioneer Company and the Willie Company in 1856), or continue to follow the North Platte (upstream) in a southwesterly direction about ten miles to a prominent landmark known as **Red Buttes.** The Martin and Hodgett Companies camped at Red Buttes, for example, when detained by the heavy snows in late October, 1856, while the Hunt Company remained at the Last Crossing of the Platte. Within a few miles the trails converged again, then proceeded southwest, past a dry area with a series of rock formations known as the **Avenue of Rocks**. Because

11

there was little water from Casper to Independence Rock, one of the most noted features between the Last Crossing of the Platte and Independence Rock was **Willow Springs**, where they found a clear, ice cold spring about ten inches deep and two feet wide, and enough grass for their livestock.

Another major landmark along this part of the trail is **Prospect Hill**, or Ryan Hill. From this spot the Pioneers could look back towards Casper, and look ahead to see the Sweetwater Mountains.

As the trail continued southwest toward Independence Rock, good water was rare. Sometimes they found water, but the water wasn't fit to drink by man or beast, which was the case at a place called **Bad Slough**. Of this area, one pioneer recorded: "Through the alkali belt, east of South Pass, their losses in cattle were enormous. Many of the men would pay no attention to the warning of the Saints, not to let their cattle drink water strongly impregnated with saleratus...As the result more than 2,000 carcasses of oxen lay strewn along the road in the alkali district, and the offensive smell made it almost impossible to travel in the vicinity."[9] Orson Hyde said: "There are three hard places for stock and teams to cross over. First, from Laramie across the Black Hills to the upper crossing of the Platte, a distance of 120 miles. The road is mostly over rocks, sharp gravel and flint. This is severe on cattle's feet.... The second hard place is from the upper crossing of the Platte to Independence Rock on the Sweetwater, a distance of fifty miles. Through this section the alkali or poisonous waters may be mostly found.... Whenever emigrants discover the road white with saleratus... they should be careful about letting their animals drink from the standing

---

[9] Little, From Kirtland to Salt Lake City, p.203.

12

pools. The third trying part of the road for stock is from the South Pass to the Green River, a distance of 65 miles. Sand and sage, sage and sand, dead horses, mules, cows, and oxen, with snow-capped mountains on your right and left, are about the variety which the eye meets in passing through this section.... [T]hose who travel this road hereafter will testify to the truth of what I have written."[10]

The Saints eventually found better water further along the trail at **Greasewood Creek** or **Sage Creek.** (Today it is known as Horse Creek.)

Independence Rock is located 48 miles southwest of Casper, Wyoming, at the far eastern end of what is called the **Sweetwater Valley.** The **Sweetwater River** may have received its name because of its clear water, compared to the alkali in much of the water available up to that point along the trail. Ezra Meeker, who crossed the plains in 1852, adds this commentary about their drinking water previous to arriving at the Sweetwater: "We had all along refused to dig little wells near the banks of the Platte, as many others did, having soon learned that the water obtained was strongly charged with alkali, while the river water was comparatively pure, other than the fine impalpable sediment, so fine as to seemingly be held in solution."

Independence Rock is 167' high on the south end, 193' high on the north end, and covers 24 acres. It is the most noted landmark along the portion of the trail west of Fort Laramie. It was a place to look for word of friends ahead or leave word for those coming on behind, and beyond those practical uses, it satisfied the human need to be known.

---

[10] As quoted in Little, From Kirtland to Salt Lake City, p. 229.

Because it was a place where many who passed by carved or painted their names, it became known as the "Register of the Desert." Although many of the Mormon Pioneers undoubtedly placed their names on the rock, the names of three saints have been identified as remaining on the rock today: Peregrine Sessions, J.W. Crosby and Bishop William Draper.

The story of the naming of the rock has only incomplete records. Lansford W. Hastings wrote in 1842: "The first party which noticed this rock was a party of American trappers who chanced to pass this way upon the Fourth of July, when, wishing to be Americans even in that secluded region of aboriginal barbarism, they proceeded to celebrate the great day which gave birth to human liberty. This they did by a succession of mountain revelings, festivities, and hilarities, which having been concluded, they all inscribed their names together with the word 'Independence' upon the most prominent and conspicuous portions of the rock, hence its name. Independence Rock thus consecrated, is destined in all coming time to stand forth as an enduring monument to civil liberty and American Independence." Velma Linford gives this honor to Ashley's men who camped here July 4, 1825.

Another historian wrote: "Asahel Munger, a missionary Oregon-bound in 1839, was told by Harris...mountain man, that the name Independence was bestowed upon it in 1830 by trappers of the American Fur Company who happened to spend the Fourth of July camped in its shadow.... The enterprising Mormons sometimes had a man or two at the Rock who would undertake to inscribe the name and date for varying prices up to five dollars, depending on location."[11]

---

[11] Paden, 1943, p.120.

In 1846, Mr. Lienhard, another emigrant bound for Oregon, wrote: "Soon we arrived at Independence Rock, known to all emigrants. I didn't measure the rock at that time, but it is perhaps one hundred feet long, forty feet wide, and thirty feet high, forming a kind of oval with rounded edges. Its sides were covered all around with names of emigrants and hunters who passed here. They reached up to such a height that it was a mystery to me how they could have put them up there. Most of the names had been painted in large letters in black or red on the brownish granite rock; only a few were carved into it. Independence Rock seemed to stand guard at the entrance to a gigantic, ancient volcanic crater."

Col. John B. Curry, who crossed in 1852, later recalled the picture of a moving wagon train viewed from the top of Independence Rock. "The wagons form a line three quarters of a mile in length. Some of the teamsters ride upon the front of their wagons, some march beside their teams, scattered along the line. Companies of women are taking exercises on foot; they gather bouquets of rare and beautiful flowers that line the way. Near them stalks the Irish wolfdog. Next comes a band of horses, two or three boys and men follow them. The docile and sagacious animals scarcely need this attention, for they have learned to follow the rear of the wagons, and know that at noon they will be allowed to graze and rest. Not so with the large herd of horned beasts that bring up the rear, lazy, selfish, and unsocial; it has been a task to get them to move."

Standing almost at the dividing line of the continent, Independence Rock was a landmark to which the emigrants directed their course, and by which they marked their western progress. The following journal entries discuss portions of the trail up to Independence Rock.

1847 Pioneer Company

April 1847, ten miles west of Winter Quarters, 1847 Pioneer Company, Comprehensive History of the Church. Elder Pratt also gave the information that Elder Taylor would arrive [from England] within a few days with the scientific instruments that had been "sent for from Winter Quarters" for use by the Pioneers, and it was resolved to await his arrival.... Elder Taylor arrived on the evening of the 13th, bringing with him the following instruments: "Two sextants, one circle of reflection, two artificial horizons, two barometers, several thermometers, telescopes, etc." The Pioneers were also furnished with maps of Captain John C. Fremont's route to California via the Great Salt Lake in 1843.

Tuesday, May 4, 1847, near North Platte, Nebraska, 1847 Pioneer Company, Wilford Woodruff Journal. *The Pioneers encountered some east-bound trappers, who encouraged them to cross and travel the better-established trail on the south side of the river, because the grass was better. Wilford Woodruff's Journal explains why they stayed on the north side of the river:* We were convinced that it would be better for us as a company to cross the river and take the old traveled road to Laramie, as there was good grass all the way on that side, while the Indians were burning it all off on the north of the river where we were traveling.[12] But when we took into consideration the situation of the next company, and the thousands that would follow, and as we were the Pioneers and had not our wives and children with us--we thought it best to keep on the north side of the river and brave the difficulties

---

[12] Some tribes had a practice of burning the prairie grasses in some places in the spring, to encourage new growth of grasses and plants that would attract buffalo herds later in the year.

of burning prairies to make a road that should stand as a permanent route for the saints independent of the then emigrant road, and let the river separate the emigrating companies that they need not quarrel for wood, grass, or water; and when our next company came along the grass would be much better for them than it would be on the south side, as it would grow up by the time they would get along; and the vote was called and it was unanimous to go on the north side of the river; so the camp again moved on.

Thursday, May 6, 1847, along the North Platte River, 1847 Pioneer Company, Orson Pratt Journal. During the time of our halts, we had to watch our teams to keep them from mingling with the buffalo. I think I may safely say that I have seen 10,000 buffalo during the day.

Saturday, May 8, 1847, along the North Platte River, Orson Pratt Journal. The prairie appeared black, being covered with buffalo.... We have seen something near 100,000 since morning.

Wednesday, May 26, 1847, near Chimney Rock, Orson Pratt Journal. In about four and three-quarter miles we arrived at the meridian of Chimney Rock, our road being about three miles to the north of it. The Platte valley is here about 3,790 feet above the level of the sea.... Grasshoppers seem to be an inhabitant of this country; I noticed that they were plenty in dry places. Prickly pears are becoming more numerous.... No buffalo seen for several days; antelope yet plentiful.

Friday, May 28, 1847, near Scottsbluff, Nebraska, 1847 Pioneer Company, William Clayton. Elder Kimball came to the next wagon where some of the boys were playing Cards. He told them his views and disapprobation of their spending time gaming, dancing, and mock trials &c. and especially the profane language frequently uttered by some. He reasoned with them on the subject and showed them that it would lead from bad to worse if persisted in until the consequences would become serious. He exhorted them to be more sober and wise.

Saturday, May 29, 1847, near Scottsbluff, Nebraska, 1847 Pioneer Company, William Clayton. After the teams were harnessed the brethren were called together... in the circle.... President Young then addressed the meeting in substance as follows:

"... Before we left Winter Quarters, it was told to the brethren that we were going to look out a home for the saints where they would be free from persecution by the gentiles, where we could dwell in peace and serve God according to the Holy Priesthood, where we could build up the Kingdom, so that the nations would begin to flock to our standard. I have said many things to the brethren, about the strictness of their walk and conduct, when we left the gentiles, and told them that we would have to walk uprightly or the law would be put in force....

"The gospel does not bind a good man down,... it is calculated to enlarge his kingdom as well as to enlarge his heart. It is calculated to give him privileges, and power, and honor, and exaltation, and everything which his heart can desire in righteousness all the days of his life....

"You can see the fruits of the spirit, but you cannot see the spirit itself with the natural eye, you behold it not. You can see the result of yielding to the evil spirit and what it will lead you to, but you do not see the spirit itself nor its operations only by the spirit that is in you....

"[U]nless there is a change and a different course of conduct, a different spirit to what is now in this Camp, I go no further. I am in no hurry. Give me the man of prayer, give me the man of faith, give me the man of meditation, a sober-minded man, and I would far rather go among the savages, with six or eight such men than to trust myself with the whole of this camp with the spirit they now possess. Here is an opportunity for every man to prove himself, to know whether he will pray and remember his God, without being asked to do it every day; to know whether he will have confidence enough to ask of God that he may receive, without my telling him to do it.... If any man had sense enough to play a game at Cards, or dance a little without wanting to keep it up all the time, but exercise a little, and then quit it and think no more of it, it would do well enough. But you want to keep it up till midnight and every night, and all the time. You don't know how to control yourselves....

"Do we suppose that we are going to look out a home for the saints, a resting place, a place of peace, where they can build up a Kingdom and bid the nations welcome, with a low, mean, dirty, trifling, covetous, wicked spirit dwelling in our bosoms? It is vain! vain!... Now let every man repent of his weaknesses, of his follies, of his meanness, and every kind of wickedness, and stop your swearing and your profane language for it is in this camp, and, I know it, and have known it."

... He then called upon all the High Priests to step forth in a line in front of the wagon, and then the Bishops to step in front of the High Priests, which being done he counted them and found their number to be 4 Bishops and 15 High Priests. He then called upon all the Seventies to form a line in the rear of the High Priests. On being counted, they were ascertained to number 78. Next he called on the Elders to form a line in the rear of the wagon. They were 8 in number. There were also 8 of the Quorum of the Twelve. He then asked the brethren of the Quorum of the Twelve, "if they were willing to covenant to turn to the Lord with all their hearts, to repent of all their follies, to cease from all their evils and serve God according to his laws." If they were willing, to manifest it by holding up their right hand. Every man held up his hand in token that he covenanted. He then put the same question to the High Priests and Bishops, next to the Seventies, and then to the Elders, and lastly to the other brethren. All covenanted with uplifted hands without a dissenting voice. He then addressed those who are not members of the Church and told them they should be protected in their rights and privileges while they would conduct themselves well, and not seek to trample on the priesthood nor blaspheme the name of God....

He then very tenderly blessed the brethren and prayed that God would enable them to fulfill their covenants and withdrew to give opportunity for others to speak if they felt like it. [Others then spoke.] President Young returned ... and said in reply, that he knew the brethren would forgive him, and the Lord will forgive us all, if we turn to Him with all our hearts and cease to do evil.

The meeting was then dismissed each man retiring to his wagon, and being half past 1 o'clock we again pursued our journey in peace, all reflecting on what has passed today, and many expressing their gratitude for what has transpired. It seemed as though we were just commencing on this important mission, and all realizing the responsibility resting upon us, to conduct ourselves in such a manner that the journey may be an everlasting blessing to us, instead of an everlasting disgrace. No loud laughter was heard, no swearing, no quarrelling, no profane language, no hard speeches to man or beast, and it truly seemed as though the cloud had burst, and we had emerged into a new element, a new atmosphere, and new society.

Wednesday, June 2, 1847, Fort Laramie, 1847 Pioneer Company, Orson Pratt Journal. By the meridian altitude of the sun, I determined the latitude of Fort Laramie to be 42 deg. 12 min. 13 sec., differing from Captain Fremont only 3 sec. of a degree, or about 8 rods. By a mean of several barometrical observations during our short stay of three days, the height of the fort above the level of the sea was calculated to be 4,090 feet.

June, 1847, Prospect Hill, 1847 Pioneer Company, William Clayton. At a quarter of a mile beyond the spring we began to ascend a very high hill which was one mile from the foot to the top and the ascent pretty steep. The summit of this hill is nicely rounding and considered to be much the highest we have traveled over. From the top can be seen a vast extent of country to the south, west and north. For about twenty or thirty miles to the south there appears to be a tolerably level bottom over which our future road runs. Beyond this there are vast ranges of high hills whose summits are spotted with snow. In the distance to the southwest can be seen a small body of water which we suppose to be a part of the Sweetwater River. To the west the ridges of rocks or hills appear nearer. They are probably not over fifteen miles from us. On the north we can see hills a long distance. The one opposite Red Buttes, near the spring where we halted yesterday noon, appears only a few miles distance. The view from this hill is one of romantic beauty which cannot easily be surpassed and as President Young remarked, would be a splendid place for a summer mansion to keep tavern. We then descended on the southwest corner of the hill and found it to be just one mile farther to the foot.

June, 1847, Greasewood [Horse] Creek, 1847 Pioneer Company, Howard Egan Journal. We crossed a stream one and three-quarters miles further, of clear water about six feet wide and one foot deep, but there is neither grass nor timber on its banks. After traveling seven miles this afternoon we turned off of the road to the left, and at 8:20 we found our camp ground, as selected by Brother Kimball, on a ridge near the above mentioned creek, about a quarter of a mile from the road. Our travel this afternoon was seven and one-quarter miles, exclusive of turning off the road, and during the day twenty miles. There is no wood and we have to use the sage roots for cooking, as it grows wild in abundance in this region. Brothers Woodruff and J. Brown went ahead this morning and have not been seen or heard of since.

June, 1847, Greasewood [Horse] Creek, 1847 Pioneer Company, William Clayton. I will here remark that it is the order of our traveling for each company of ten to go forward in their turn. The first ten in the first division taking the lead one day, then on the second day it falls in the rear of the first division, the second ten takes the lead and this continues till each company of ten have taken the lead one day a piece. Then the first division falls in the rear of the second division which also begins by companies of ten to take the lead of the road as stated above and when each ten have had their day, the second division again falls in the rear of the first which continues in the same order. Thus every man has his equal privilege of traveling one with another. After traveling two and a half miles we descended to the bottom land again and saw a small stream a little to the left of the road where there is plenty of grass. One and three-quarters miles farther we crossed a creek of tolerably clear water about six feet wide, and one foot deep, but neither grass nor timber on its banks. After traveling seven miles this afternoon we turned off the road to the left and at 8:20 formed our encampment on a ridge near the last mentioned creek where there is good feed, having traveled this afternoon seven and a quarter miles, exclusive of allowance for turning from the road, and during the day twenty miles. We had been in hopes of reaching the Sweetwater but it appears we are yet some miles from it. The whole country around is entirely destitute of timber, not a tree to be seen, nor a shrub larger than the wild sage which abounds in all this region of country and will answer for cooking when nothing else can be found. Some anxiety is felt on account of the absence of Elder Woodruff and John Brown. They started ahead this morning with instructions to go on about fifteen miles and if they found a good place to camp, to stay. They have not been seen or heard of since. It is supposed they have fallen in with some of the companies either forward or back and have concluded to tarry with them over night.

June, 1847, From Willow Springs to Independence Rock, 1847 Pioneer Company, Wilford Woodruff. President Young wished me to go on about 15 miles and look up a camp ground for the night, so I went forward. George A. Smith went with me to the head of the Willow Springs. We there found a doctor belonging to a Missouri company who had been doctoring a sick family in a company that was forward. He was of the opinion that the Willow Springs were still ten miles ahead, which was incorrect as he was then sitting at the head of them. Brother Smith stopped with the doctor to wait for our wagons to come up, and I rode on alone. After traveling several miles Brother John Brown came up with me and we rode on together over a sandy, barren, sage country to a creek of good water containing some small fish about ten miles west of the Willow Springs. We arrived here at half past one o'clock and turned out our horses to bait. We tarried until four o'clock watching for our company to come in sight, but we could see no wagons. We saw two horsemen approaching us, so we waved a small flag for them to come to us. We supposed they were some of our company, but they were two hunters, Captain Smith and another man from the Missouri company carrying in buffalo meat to their camp. They thought we were Indians in the distance and made off.

I mounted my horse and put after them and soon overtook them and made inquiries about our camp. They said they had not seen it, but had seen a company of about a dozen wagons coming by themselves. I then concluded our camp had stopped by the Willow Springs. So Captain Smith who was the leader of the Missouri company invited us to go on and camp with them for the night, as they did not expect to go but a few miles farther than the creek we were now on. As it was five o'clock and we could see five miles on the road back and no wagons in sight I concluded that our company would not come and if they should they would go no farther than the creek, so we accepted Captain Smith's proposal and went on with him to spend the night with his camp. But instead of his going but a little distance he continued on mile after mile and could neither find feed or water, except the salt and alkali ponds and lakes until we struck the Sweetwater River at Independence Rock which is so noted in Fremont's Journal and other travelers, which was 12 miles west of the creek before spoken of. Their oxen had tired out having traveled about 27 miles and much of the road was very sandy and we had rode about 30 miles and was quite weary. The Sweetwater is truly sweet to man and beast after traveling through so much ground covered with salt, potash and alkali water as is found on the way. We turned out our horses in good feed, got supper, which was bacon, buffalo, corn bread, coffee, milk, etc., then lay down upon the ground and spent the night under a tent with the Missourians, but did not rest well. *I found a great difference between the Missouri emigrant companies and our own, for while the men, women and children were all cursing, swearing, quarreling, scolding and finding fault with each other and other companies, there was nothing of the kind allowed or practiced in our own camp.* But to return to our camp I will say at a late hour they came up to the creek that we left back 12 miles, [Greasewood Creek] and the grass being poor we continued on four miles west of the creek and camped for the night. They traveled 20 miles while I traveled 30 miles. The camp not finding me at the creek, nor hearing from me at all felt some alarm lest I was lost, or got into trouble with the Indians or some difficulty, they blew their bugle and watched for me until midnight and finally fired their cannon while I was camped ten miles from them not thinking I was giving them any trouble. [Emphasis added.]

June, 1847, Independence Rock, 1847 Pioneer Company, William Clayton. Independence Rock and ford--on the north side of the river--about six hundred yards long, and a hundred and twenty wide, composed of soft granite.... The rock Independence lies a little west of where we have halted and after dinner I went to view it as well as many others. It lies on the north bank of the river in this shape: The extreme southeast corner reaches to within about three rods of the river and runs in a direction northwest while the river at this place runs nearly a west course. It is composed of the same barren granite as other masses in this region and is probably 400 yards long, 80 yards wide and 100 yards in perpendicular height as near as I could guess. The ascent is difficult all around. Travelers appear to have ascended it mostly at the southeast corner where there are some hundreds of names of persons who have visited it, both male and female, painted on the projecting surfaces with black, red and some with yellow paint. About half way up there is a cavern about twelve feet long and three feet wide at the bottom but at the top about ten feet wide and eight feet high, formed by a very large heavy mass of rock having sometime fallen over an opening or cavity, leaving scarcely room enough for a man to enter. However there are three places by which it may be entered though not without difficulty. there are a number of names inside the cavern put on with black paint, doubtless being the names of persons who have visited it. On the top of the rock the surface is a little rounding, something like a large mound with large masses of loose rock lying scattered around. Proceeding forward you descend, when nearly half way of the length, to a considerably lower surface which continue some distance and then rises high again to about the same height as the first section. On the top there are a number of small pools of water, no doubt collected during heavy rains and having no chance to run off, they stand until evaporated into the atmosphere.

June 21, 1847, Independence Rock, 1847 Pioneer Company, Wilford Woodruff. I arose early this morning, took breakfast and in company with Brother Brown, we rode clear around Independence Rock. I should judge the distance to be about 3/4 of a mile, we examined the many names and lists of names of the trappers, traders, travelers, and immigrants which are painted upon these rocks. Nearly all the names were put on with red, black, and yellow paint, some had washed out and the greatest number was put on within a few years. Some of them were quite plain, of about 30 years.... After going around and examining it, we staked our horses, mounted the rock, and I went forward and gained the highest point at the south end of the rock, which contained the names.... After examining it, I went to the north end, which is the highest part of the rock, here is an opening or cavern that would contain 30 or 40 persons and a rock...the highest peak of about 3 tons weight. We got upon this rock and offered up our prayers, according to the order of the priesthood, we prayed... for the blessings of God to rest upon President Young and his brethren of the Twelve and all of the pioneer camp and the whole camp of Israel and House of Israel, over our wives and children and relatives, the Mormon Battalion, all the churches abroad, and that the Lord would hasten the time of the fulfillment of his promises to Abraham, Isaac, Jacob, Joseph, Lehi, Nephi, Alma, and Moroni and all the sayings of the Lord concerning the building up of Zion in the last days and avenging the blood of the prophets and while offering up our prayer the spirit of the Lord descended upon us and we truly felt to rejoice and while we were attending to our prayers, the Missourians were burying a woman a little distance from the Rock by the name of Rachel Morgan, 25 years of age.... After surveying the Rock, what we wished, we again descended to the ground. I was the first Latter-day Saint that ever went to that rock and offered up prayers according to the order of the priesthood.

Willie Handcart Company, 1856

Thursday, May 1, 1856, Liverpool, England, Willie Company Journal. The passengers arrived at the dock and boarded the Thornton. They took possession of their berths as allotted to them. By evening, order and tranquility prevailed throughout the whole ship. On this day, Jennet McNeil from Haddington, Edinborough, England, had a baby boy at 5:00 p.m. The number of passengers are as follows: 560 adults, 172 children, 29 infants.

Wednesday, May 7, 1856, aboard the Thornton, Willie Company Journal. Passengers still suffering sea sickness. The greatest order prevailed on board, everyone seemed to respect the rights of each other, and to obey those placed to preside over them. Sister Rachel Curtis, aged 75 years, died of old age, being declining before she left Liverpool, at 7:30 p.m. She was from Norton, Gloucestershire. In the different wards prayers were offered up mornings and evenings, and to be continued during the voyage. Light airs, cloudy weather.

Thursday, May 8, 1856, aboard the Thornton, Willie Company Journal. This morning sea sickness remained, though gradually recovering. At 10:00 a.m. the bell tolled, a signal that the hour had arrived when we were to consign the remains of our beloved Sister Curtis to the sea to await the resurrection of the just. Great solemnity prevailed among all present. President Willie offered up a prayer to the Almighty. She was buried in the mighty deep.

May and June, 1856, aboard the Thornton, Willie Company Journal. *The journal records a total of seven deaths at sea, three marriages, one birth, and four babies blessed.*

Saturday, June 14, 1856, New York City, Willie Company Journal. This morning a clear sky and favorable wind.... At 8 a.m. steamboat Achilles cam along side. We were towed to New york. General stir among the passengers, all getting ready to land; good feeling prevailing. Doctor came on board off Staten Island and gave a certificate of the good health of the passengers. The custom house also came and passed our luggage without any inspection. At sun down, we landed at the Castle Garden, a large building appropriated for emigrants, where we were visited by Elder Felt who kindly welcomed us.

Thursday, June 26, 1856, Iowa City, Iowa, Willie Company Journal. *The group had traveled by railroad from New York City, by steamboat on Lake Erie, and by railroad to the Mississippi River in Illinois.* This morning at 7 a.m., we left and crossed the Mississippi by the steam ferry boat, and at 9 a.m. we left by rail for Iowa City. We arrived there at 1:30 p.m., and camped on the green, but in consequence of a thunderstorm approaching, we obtained possession of a large engine shed and remained there during the night, it raining in torrents all night. Many of the brethren from the camp visited and cordially welcomed us, and on their return, took a large number of the sisters to the camp with them.

Saturday, June 28, 1856, Iowa City, Iowa, Willie Company Journal. The Saints were all cheerful and happy, and under the circumstances, doing the best they could without tents. President Willie received instruction from President D. Spencer to continue in charge of the company for the time being. The sisters were busily engaged in making tents, under the direction of Elder William Ledingham.... General good feeling prevailing amongst the Saints, and all appear to desire to hearken to the counsel of those over them. Everybody in the camp appeared to be busy making handcarts, yokes, etc. for the trip across the plains. This evening it commenced to rain very heavy. *The Saints bore it with fortitude, perfectly resigned to the will of Heaven. Union and love seem to prevail with all.* [Emphasis added.]

1856, From Iowa to Wyoming, Willie Company, Jens Nielson.[13] Upon arriving at the end of the railroad in Iowa, Jens Nielson obtained a victory which to most of us is the most difficult of all, that of parting with money and security. He had the money from the sale of his farm, and unboastfully stated in a letter to his son that he, Jens, had let all of his money go to the Church except enough to buy a handcart, and to stock it with 15 pounds of belongings per person. Thus, he could have obtained wagons, horses, stacks of food and other supplies and traveled west in style and comfort, and early enough to beat the winter. He gained the great victory over selfishness by parting with his life's savings and demonstrated his unyielding faith so that Saints who had nothing might at least have a handcart. Jens quoted: "Obedience is better than sacrifice." Jens, Elsiek, their 6 year old son, and a young Bodil Mortensen girl, for whom the assumed responsibility to bring to Utah, were left with a handcart, poorly constructed of green lumber, and unfit for the journey. Jens was placed in a camp with four other men with their families who spoke a strange language, English, which Jens could not understand. Jens was made captain of this camp in the Willie handcart company. The company was late starting, and delayed by

---

[13] The events included here that pertain to Jens Nielson are as quoted in Glorious Victory, by Jay P. Nielson.

repeated breakdowns of the poorly constructed handcarts. When finally reaching Wyoming's wind-swept plains, they were caught in a very early and severe winter, with two feet of snow, temperatures to eleven degrees below zero and howling blizzard winds.

1856, Iowa City, Iowa, Willie Company, William James History.[14] It was now six weeks since the companies had arrived at Camp Iowa, Emma James remembers. "We were called together in a meeting one evening and there was quite a bit of guessing as to the reason for it. It was a large group that gathered, circling the leader. The meeting was called to order, one of the brethren offered prayer, then we were told for the reason for the counseling. We were told it was 300 miles to Council Bluffs which was the actual place for starting the trek and that was just a mile to what we had to go to reach the valley. We would have carts, such as they were, but the season was late and bad weather could prove dangerous to us if we were in the mountains. Even if we had no trouble, we would be late getting to Utah. There had been much talk of these dangers by experienced men in the camp, but I think that the thing which I will remember for the rest of my life and wish that we had heeded was said by a Brother Savage. With tears streaming down his cheeks he pleaded with the people, 'Brothers and sisters, wait until spring to make this journey. Some of the strong may get through in case of bad weather, but the bones of the weak and old will strew the way.' I can remember that when he finished there was a long time of silence. I was frightened. Father looked pale and sick. I turned to Mother to see what she was thinking, and all that I saw was her old determined look. She was ready to go on

---

[14] All accounts included in this book that relate to William James are taken from the History of William James, written by his descendant Laleta Dickson.

tomorrow. There were many others like her. We really didn't have much choice. There was no work here for us to keep ourselves through the winter, and our family had to live. 'We must always put our trust in the Lord', said Mother, and that was that.

"There was nearly one hundred people of the companies who decided to winter over and come in the spring. The majority voted to go on as soon as everything was ready. July 15th, under the direction of Captain Willy, with 500 people, 120 carts and four or five wagons we left Camp Iowa for an outfitting station at Council Bluffs. It was great fun pulling empty carts and imitating the wagon drivers with their 'eeh' and 'hah'."

July, 1856, Iowa City, Willie Company, John Chislett Journal.[15] Levi Savage stated that they "could not cross the mountains with a mixed company of aged people, women, and little children, so late in the season without much suffering, sickness, and death." He therefore advised going into winter quarters without delay. Savage was voted down, the majority being against him. He then added: "Brethren and sisters, what I have said I know to be true; but seeing you are to go forward, I will go with you, will help you all I can, will work with you, will rest with you, will suffer with you, and, if necessary, I will die with you. May God in his mercy bless and preserve us."

Tuesday, July 15, 1856, Iowa City, Iowa, Willie Company Journal. We finished weighing the luggage today. Sister Eliza Hurren was delivered of a daughter about 6 a.m. yesterday; also Franklin Richins was born this day, to John and

---

[15] All references to the John Chislett Journal are quotations as included in T.B.H. Stenhouse, Rocky Mountain Saints.

31

Charlotte Richins of the Cheltenham Conference, and Richard Godfrey, of Worcester Conference was joined in matrimony to Ann Herbert of the same Branch, by Bishop Tyler.[16] We started out a short distance this day and encamped for the night. All in first rate spirits.

July, 1856, Iowa, Willie Company Journal. *The journal tells of over fifteen members of the company who turned back within the first ten days after leaving Iowa City.*

Friday, July 25, 1856, Muddy Creek, Iowa, Willie Company Journal. Traveled as far as Muddy Creek, 13 miles. Stopped twice by the way to rest. The weather being very warm. Just before we camped, we were overtaken by the Sheriff with a warrant to search the wagons, under the idea that the women were detained contrary to their wishes, with ropes. After showing their authority, they had permission to examine any part of the company, and were fully satisfied that the report was without foundation, and they left us.

Thursday, July 31, 1856, Des Moines, Iowa, Willie Company Journal. Crossed on the Flat Boat Bridge and passed about a mile through the town, where we stopped till 2 o'clock to give the cattle water and grass. We pursued our journey again about 4 miles, where we encamped for the night. Mr. Charles Good, a respectable gentleman from the City, who seemed very favorable to the Gospel, from no impure motive, brought a present of 15 pairs of childrens boots.

Tuesday, August 12, 1856, Florence, Nebraska, Willie Company Journal. This morning the brethren are busy

----

[16] From the Willie Company's arrival in America to the date they started the trek from Iowa City, the Company Journal speaks of four additional births, five deaths, two baptisms, and one marriage.

getting the Saints to sign bonds; finding out who intends stopping, what hand-carts want repairing, with many other things which are requisite before proceeding on our journey across the plains. In the evening, Brother McGaw and Brother Willie addressed the Saints and gave them some needful instructions and advice before proceeding on the remainder of the journey.

1856, along the Platte River and the North Platte in Nebraska and Wyoming, Willie Company, John Chislett Journal. We started from Florence about the 18th of August, and travelled in the same way as through Iowa, except that our carts were more heavily laden, as our teams could not haul sufficient flour to last us to Utah; it was therefore decided to put one sack (ninety-eight pounds) on each cart in addition to the regular baggage. Some of the people grumbled at this, the majority bore it without a murmur. Our flour ration was increased to a pound per day; fresh beef was issued occasionally, and each "hundred" had three or four milch cows. The flour on the carts was used first, the weakest parties being the first relieved of their burdens.

Everything seemed to be propitious, and we moved gaily forward full of hope and faith. At our camp each evening could be heard songs of joy, merry peals of laughter, and bon mots on our condition and prospects. Brother Savage's warning was forgotten in the mirthful ease of the hour. The only drawbacks to this part of our journey were the constant breaking down of carts and the delays caused by repairing them. The axles and boxes being of wood, and being ground out by the dust that found its way there in spite of our efforts to keep it out, together with the extra weight put on the carts, had the effect of breaking the axles at the shoulder. All kinds of expedients were resorted to as remedies for the growing evil, but with variable success. Some wrapped their axles with leather obtained from bootlegs; others with tin, obtained by sacrificing tin-plates, kettles, or buckets from their mess outfit. Besides these inconveniences, there was felt a great lack of a proper lubricator. Of anything suitable for this purpose we had none at all. The poor folks had to use their bacon (already totally insufficient for their wants) to grease their axles, and some even used their soap, of which they had very little, to make their carts trundle somewhat easier.

We reached [Fort] Laramie about the 1st or 2nd of September, but the provisions, etc., which we expected, were not there for us. Captain Willie called a meeting to take into consideration our circumstances, conditions, and prospects, and to see what could be done. It was ascertained that at our present rate of travel and consumption of flour the latter would be exhausted when we were about three hundred and fifty miles from our destination. It was resolved to reduce our allowance from one pound to three-quarters of a pound per day, and at the same time to make every effort in our power to travel faster. We continued this rate of rations from Laramie to Independence Rock.

1856, From Iowa to Wyoming, Willie Company, William James History. We got away ahead of the slow wagons and had to wait for them. We had plenty of time to see the country we were passing through--to run here and there and explore. There were many things to catch the eye in a strange land.

At Council Bluffs the company outfitted for the journey West. It was organized much the same as the wagon trains had been. Captains were placed over hundreds, fifties, etc. The Saints were put on a strict schedule. Each member had his chores for the company as well as for his own family. The strong were to pull the carts. Everyone over seven years of age was expected to walk. The very old and the very young could ride. The young men were expected to act as herders for the cattle. Rueben James was one of these. The young women and girls were expected to look after the children who were walking and to gather in the fuel for the camp at night. The girls in the James family had their chores. Sarah and Emma took turns with their parents in pulling the carts. Maryann and Martha watched over their little brother George. John Parley rode in the cart. Maryann tells of what fun they had. She says, "when we started out on the trail each morning there was always something new to see. Maybe it was a bird running along the road which we chased but never did catch. There was always flowers and pretty rocks to pick. This land was so different from the one in England that it kept us interested. We were constantly being warned not to get too far away from the trail, but I can't remember that we heeded the warning until we had one or two experiences which made us more careful.

"One day as we were skipping along side the carts and singing, where we was always happiest as I remember it, a group of Indians on horseback rode up and followed along with us for a while. We didn't know the Redman well enough to be too friendly, so we quieted down and stayed close to our parents. One of the Indians seemed fascinated by the contraptions being pulled along by people. Finally his curiosity got the best of him. He leaped off his horse, ran over to one of the carts which was being pulled by a women and her daughter and gave it such a hard push that it nearly ran over them. The women and girl screamed and got out of the shafts as fast as they could. The Indian pushed the cart a little ways, and apparently satisfied, he jumped on his horse and rode off. He, with some of his friends, came back later to beg food. We gave it to them because we were told that the Indians were our brethren and that we should treat them so. We never did have any trouble with them except that they never seem to learn that it is stealing to take something that didn't belong to them.

"Another incident was to cause the timid and even the impulsive to watch wearily for dust clouds and small black specks in the distance which could prove a menace very quickly. One evening as we prepared to stop fo. he night, a large load of buffalo came thundering towards us. It sounded like thunder at first, then the big black animals came straight for our carts. We were so scared that we were rooted to the ground. One of the Captains, seeing what was going on, ran for the carts which was still coming in, jerked out some of the carts to make a path for the steady stream of animals and let them go through. They went past us like a train roaring along. I am sure that but for the quick thinking of these men, many of us would have been trampled to death. The animals acted as if they were crazy the way they ran. We hoped that we wouldn't meet such a large herd soon again. After they had gone somebody called out that the cattle had gone with them. This was our only supply of meat, so the men started to ride out after them. The men on foot soon lost sight of the herd. Those of us who were left made preparation for the night hoping the men would be back with our cattle by dark. As the sun went down, a terrible storm came up. A strong wind tore the tents out of our hands and sent everything flying in all directions. The thunder and lightning was like nothing we had ever seen before. We had all we could do to keep track of each other. The noise terrified the children so that they ran for any shelter they could find. Soon we all did for the rain came down in torrents, and in a matter of minutes we were soaked to the skin. The men came in from the hunt empty handed but in time to gather up our belongings and get ready for our meal. We all went to bed wet and cold.

"The cattle were never found, even the tracks were washed away by the rain. This was to prove a serious thing for the company. With no oxen or mules to pull the wagons, it was necessary to hitch the milk cows to the wagons. It was a sorry group which started out on the trail the next morning. Now was the time when they needed the special song, so they sang as they trudged through the mud, 'for some must push and some must pull as we go marching up the hill, for merrily,

merrily on we go until we reach the valley-o.'" Maryann James said that that was a wonderful song, and she sang it as loud as she could.

It was now September and heavy frost lay on the ground in the morning. The roads were deeply rutted from the storms and frost and it made it hard to walk for those who had poor shoes or none at all. The carts which had been giving trouble from the start were breaking down regularly and causing delays along the way. Rawhide was used to hold parts together, but the green wood gave trouble, especially the axle.... Most of the party did not realize the seriousness of the situation, but Captain Willy and his Captains were well aware of it. William James was concerned. He had talked to some of the women who were familiar with the country. Quietly, but with fear in his heart, he worked harder to keep his cart in repair so there would be no delays....

Flour was rationed to 6 oz. per day per person, and there wasn't much to go with it. Many were weakening from the lack of nourishing food. The young and the old and the weak began to die quietly. Even the strong men, who were secretly giving their portion to families, pulled their carts until they died. Soon rations were cut again. Clothing was in rags, especially shoes. Any piece of rag, burlap or canvas was tied around the feet. All too soon this was chewed through by the torturous terrain.

1856, From Iowa to Wyoming, Willie Company, George Cunningham Journal. I think that it is written somewhere that the devil is prince and power of the air. If so, he must have been in an awful rage; for such storms continued for several successive nights. Of course, some growled and repined about the good homes they had left. Indeed, many felt like the ancient Israelites who looked back and moaned after their leeks and onions of Egypt. But after a few days, cloth was procured and tents were made and things went along much better. We camped here five or six weeks before we could get away. At last we were told we were to go in Brother Willy's handcart company. This company consisted of about 600 persons, men, women and children. There were 100 Scotch, 200 Danes, and about 300 English. A captain was appointed over each 100, he being chosen from the returning missionaries. One team was appointed to haul provisions for each 100. The cattle were wild and the teamsters were green but we got along the best we could. We had 300 miles to travel right through Iowa before we could reach the permanent starting place, Winter Quarters or Florence. While traveling along, people would mock, sneer, and deride us on every occasion for being such fools as they termed us, and would often throw out inducements to get us to stop. But we told them we were going to Zion, and would not stop on any account. When we went through a town or settlement pulling our handcarts as we always had to do, people would turn out in crowds to laugh at us, crying "gee-haw" as if we were oxen. But this did not discourage us in the least, for we knew that we were on the right track. That was enough.

After several weeks pulling, hauling and praying, we arrived in Florence, but were detained again several weeks more. Some stayed here, and would not go on any further. In fact, we were told that if any wanted to stop, they might do so, but the council was to go on to the Valleys. I can remember the opening at a meeting one night when Brother Levi Savage, a returning missionary rose and spoke. He counseled the old, weak and sickly to stop until another spring. The tears commenced to flow down his cheeks and he prophesied that if such undertook the journey at that late season of the year, that their bones would strew the way.

At length we started but our number was greatly reduced. About 100 stayed who would not go any further. I must state that there was not one of our 100 stopped, for that we got the praise. The ox teams were loaded down and we were delayed much by having to wait on them. We strove along daily and when we got to Wood River, we came across a large camp of Omaha Indians who were very friendly. They invited us to camp with them for a night. We did so.... [As] we traveled up the flat, [we] saw immense herds of buffalo. Some places the prairie was black with them, there were so many. We could not keep them out of the train while traveling. We killed some of them and had plenty of meat. Some felt like wasting it because it was so plentiful. I saw a man who had one. Went and cut a few pieces out of the carcass and let the balance go to waste.

It happened like this as soon as we flung camp, one of those terrible storms blew up which are only known in a prairie country.[17] Every man ran to help put up the tents, and the

---

[17] It was in this same vicinity, between Iowa City, Iowa and Florence, Nebraska, that the McArthur Handcart Company (the second handcart company of 1856, who started early enough to avoid any significant problems) encountered a rainstorm on July 1, 1856. "Robert and Ann Parker were traveling in McArthur's Company with their four children: Max, 12; Martha Alice, 10; Arthur, 6; and Ada, 1 year old. One day little Arthur sat down to rest, unnoticed by the other children. A sudden storm came up, and the company hurriedly made camp. Finding that Arthur was not with the children, an organized search was begun. It continued a second day, but without success. 'Ann Parker pinned a bright shawl about the thin shoulders of her husband and sent him back alone on the trail to search again for their child. If he found him dead, he was to wrap him in the shawl; if alive, the shawl would be a flag to signal her. Ann and her children took up their load and struggled on with the company, while Robert retraced the miles of forest trail, calling, and searching and praying for his helpless little son. At last he reached a mail and trading station where he learned that his child had been found and cared for by a woodsman and his wife. He had been ill from exposure and fright. But God had heard the prayers of his people. Out on the trail each night Ann and her children kept watch and,

cattle guard ran to save the women and children also, thinking that the storm would subside after a little and they would tend to their cattle again, but it kept up the whole night, and it soon became dark as pitch and all hands had to hold on to the tents to keep them from going down. The pioneers were flooded in a few moments, the thunder roared most deafeningly, a captive of the most vivid flashes of light in which seemed to electrify everything.

"The lightning flashed from pole to pole.

Near and more near the thunder rolled."

Have you ever read the Southey's poem, "How the Water Comes Down at Lodore"?, or did you ever read of the ancient Roman artist who went to a victorious general to buy one of his prisoners of war for the purpose of putting him to death by inches that he might cultivate his art on the agonies of death. Oh for the pen of the thought, oh for the brush of the artist. Had they been there! But such thoughts are above the power of pen to describe. How must it be with a mariner that is lashed to the helm, while the seas wash all around him, when it is so difficult to stand such a storm on terra-firma. Thoughts like this and similar ones seem to give us purpose and strength until morning came. [During the storm most of the company's oxen stampeded with a buffalo herd. The men hunted for them, but recovered very few.]

It was evident to all that our provisions were getting very short. We had between six and seven hundred miles to travel to accomplish our journey, which we would be compelled to do or perish in the mountain snows. We therefore came to the conclusion to take the provisions out of the wagons and put them on the handcarts. We had about

---

when, on the third night, the rays of the setting sun caught the glimmer of a bright red shawl, the brave little mother sank, in a pitiful heap in the sand. . . Ann slept for the first time in 6 days.'"
Hafen, Handcarts to Zion, pp. 63-64.

thirty milk cows which we hitched on to the wagons to haul the sick. The children who were not able to walk were put on the handcarts also, and we who were able had to haul them. Here we plodded along through the mud with all the courage that we could muster. Our bright young sisters helped us by doing all they could to encourage us in every shape, and whenever an opportunity afforded, they would try to cheer us along with their beautiful strains of vocal music. They seemed to have songs very appropriate for every occasion. This was much help to us under stiff circumstances. Some of their words I can well remember yet such as:

"Some will push and some will pull,
As we go marching up the hill,
So merrily on the way we go
Until we reach the valley-o."

They used to sing also the following words a great deal:

"Hooray for the camp of Israel,
Hooray for the handcarts scheme,
Hooray, hooray, it's better by far
Than the wagon and ox-team...."

We went along slowly and after a few weeks more arrived at Fort Laramie. As the provisions were very exhausted our Captain went to Fort Laramie and bought tenth or two of flour for which he had to pay $20.00 per hundred pounds. After leaving, we were met by a company of missionaries going to the States. Elder Parley P. Pratt came and talked a while to us and tried to encourage us. The nights now began to be very cold and the seed was very poor. Our provisions were running out fast. Starvation looked us in the face. We were put on rations of 6 ozs. of flour per day and nothing else. The old and the weak began to die off, and a great many of the young and strong soon followed suit. We were several weeks on this small ration. They called us together, and said that all the provisions were gone, except some few crackers which he had saved for the sick and the small children. There were only one or two hundred pounds of them. He said that all hands would be treated alike; that he would kill every critter in the train before any of us would die of starvation.

Friday, September 12, 1856, near North Platte, Nebraska, Willie Company Journal. Pursuant to a previous threat or promise, Captain Atwood pulled down a tent or two this morning (about an hour and a half after the horn had blown), exposing the serene features of its sleeping inmates, much to their chagrin, and the amusement of bystanders. Some of the sleepers wanted to draw the tent back over them as a covering, but it was a "no go" ....

This evening President Franklin D. Richards ... arrived just before dusk in 3 carriages and 2 wagons.... President Richards then addressed the Saints, expressing his satisfaction at their having journeyed thus far, and more especially with handcarts, and ... which he knew had proved, and would prove their salvation, if they would hearken to, and diligently obey counsel to the letter. In which even, he promised, in the name of Israel's God, and by the authority of the Holy Priesthood, that no obstacle whatever should come in the way of this camp, but what they should be able, by their united faith and works, to overcome, God being their helper. And, that if a Red Sea should interpose, they should by their union of heart and hand, walk through it like Israel of old, dryshod. On the same conditions, he promised that though they might have some trials to endure as proof to God, and the brethren, that they had the true "grit."

Saturday, September 20, 1856, near Ash Hollow, Nebraska, Willie Company Journal. This morning Sister Stewart stated that when she descended into Ash Hollow instead of turning to the right towards the river where our camp was, she turned to the left because she saw a road in that direction. She went for a long distance on such a road, and not seeing anything of the camp, turned back to the place where we nooned yesterday. She slept last night on the bluffs of the open prairie, and she was followed by some wolves, one of which came within 2 yards of her. I seemed inclined to be rather too familiar, which she instantly checked by a steady gaze, accompanied by an authoritative shake or wave of her right hand.

Wednesday, October 1, 1856, Fort Laramie, Willie Company Journal. The handcart company rolled out, then turned back to an elevated spot of ground commanding a full view of the fort. The first thing this morning, it was discovered that several sisters had left the camp and had taken up their residence at the fort. Early this morning, Brother David Reeder died, aged 54.

Wednesday, October 1, 1856, Fort Laramie, Willie Company, Joseph B. Elder Journal. We reached Fort Laramie about the first of October quite a fussing in camp sum grunted sum lyed and sum apostatized sum followed us after we was gone and beged the captain to receive them again into the company we moved on better than we antisipated under the circumstances for we had fine weather only one storm all the way up the Plat and I do not believe we would have had that had it not been for sum of the mean conduct of sum of the company. [Original spelling retained.]

Thursday, October 2, 1856, near Fort Laramie, Willie Company, William Woodward, Clerk. Several missionaries came into camp this morning. Among them was Thomas Bullock and several others. They were in good spirits. Several brethren went to their wagons, as they were traveling, and Brother Parley P. Pratt came to our camp and preached a discourse, suitable to the times, which was well received by the people. He finally bid the camp goodbye, and went on his way

43

to the States. Brother Willie accompanied him to Fort Laramie. The camp rolled on as usual, and traveled about 7 miles and camped. A meeting was held in the evening, where Brothers Willie, Atwood, and Savage addressed them on the necessity of shortening the rations of the camp, so that our flour might hold out till supplies should meet us. The people were willing to listen to Captain Willie's suggestion, and it was unanimously approved by the people.

Friday, October 10, 1856, Casper, Willie Company, William Woodward, Clerk. We called at the trading post[18] and obtained 37 buffalo robes for the use of the handcart company, which had been engaged by brother F.D. Richards. Traveled about 6 miles and nooned. Rolled on again and forded the Platte River [at the Last Crossing] and camped on its banks. Traveled about 12 miles through the day.

Monday, October 13, 1856, Greasewood [Horse] Creek, Willie Company, William Woodward, Clerk. The camp rolled on, passed the "Willow Springs," ascended "Prospect Hill," and nooned at a "Bad Slough." Rolled on to "Greasewood Creek" & camped for the night. Travelled about 13 miles. Paul Jacobsen, from Lolland Denmark, aged 55 died this evening.

October, 1856, Greasewood [Horse] Creek, Willie Company, Jens Pederson Journal. On October 12th, Capt. Willie was forced to cut their rations again, this time to 10 oz. for men, 9 for women, 6 for children, and 3 for infants. Their last flour was used on October 19th and that night the first snow fell.

---

[18] The trading post was located at a place called "Richard's Bridge."

Tuesday, October 14, 1856, Independence Rock, Willie Company, William Woodward, Clerk. Weather splendid. Road sandy. Rolled on to the Saleratus Lake & nooned. Traveled on, & the Handcarts with the people crossed the Sweetwater River on a bridge. The teams & wagons forded the stream. Camped about a mile west of "Independence Rock." Came about 13 miles. The people gathered considerable saleratus from a lake on the left of the road east of Independence Rock of superior quality.

Martin Handcart Company, 1856

Sunday, June 29, 1856, aboard the Horizon anchored in Massachusetts Bay, Martin Company, John Jaques Journal. On the 29th, the passengers passed the doctor. A meeting was held on deck, and in the response to three cheers, for the captain, he complimented the passengers on their good behavior and said that company was the best he had ever brought across the sea. He further said that since the passengers sang, "We'll marry none but Mormons," he would "carry none but Mormons."

Sunday, July 20, 1856, Iowa City, Martin Company (with the Hodgett Company), Jesse Haven Journal. Wrote a letter to my wife, also to Brother and Sister Shefford of Afton, Illinois, and my sister in the state of Massachusetts. Attended meeting in the afternoon and preached a few moments, bore my testimony of Joseph Smith being a prophet of the Most High. Felt well. About dark, noticed that my company must get away as soon as possible.

Tuesday, July 22, 1856, Iowa City, Martin Company, (with the Hodgett Company) Jesse Haven Journal. The weather is hot, the thermometer in the tent stood at 108 degrees between 5 and 6 p.m. My company started, went about a mile, then camped for the night. I called them together and gave them some instructions, then to the main camp.

July, 1856, Iowa City, Martin Company, John Jaques Journal. As only a very limited amount of baggage could be taken with the handcarts, during the long stay on the Iowa City camping ground, there was a general lightening of such things as could best be done without. Many things were sold cheaply to residents of that vicinity, and many more things were left on the camping ground for anybody to take or leave at his pleasure. I was grievous to see the heaps of books and other articles thus left in the sun, rain, and dust, representing a respectable amount of money spent therefor in England, but thenceforth, a waste and dead loss to the proper owners.

Wednesday, July 30, 1856, Iowa Territory, Martin Company (with the Hodgett Company), Jesse Haven Journal. This morning at prayers, we disfellowshipped Emma Batchelor, who left us yesterday and went out among the gentiles to tarry there. Traveled today about 9 miles. Brother Robert Evans and Sarah White, came to me and wished to be excused from going any further because he, Robert Evans, was out of health. I excused them. As we came into camp, we broke a yoke. I set two of the brethren to make another.

Friday, August 1, 1856, Iowa Territory, Martin Company (with the Hodgett Company), Jesse Haven Journal. This morning, I learned that 3 or 4 left the camp last night; one woman and her child and other children, whose mother died since we started on our journey. We traveled 6 miles today. Two families talk of leaving and wish to get my counsel. To do so, at the last, I told one of them he might do as he thought proper, and I would not disfellowship him for it. I had established the rule, if any left the camp without counsel, they should be disfellowshipped from the church. Brother Moses left today with his family, also Brother Hunter and his family. Saints complain that the provisions provided is not sufficient for them. Some dissatisfaction on account of it. Traveled only a few miles today. The day is hot.

Thursday, August 7, 1856, Iowa Territory, Martin Company, Samuel Openshaw Journal. We started about 7 o'clock this morning and traveled through a beautiful country, where we could stand and gaze upon the prairies as far as the eye could see, even until the prairies themselves seemed to meet the sky on all sides, without being able to see a house. I thought, how many thousands of people are there in England who have scarce room to breathe and not enough to eat. Yet all this good land is lying dormant, except for the prairie grass to grow and decay. We traveled about 15 miles

Saturday, August 9, 1856, Iowa Territory, Martin Company (with the Hodgett Company), Jesse Haven Journal. Started early and traveled 10 miles, then camped on the Middle Coon River.... Saints traveled badly today. Much problems after we got into camp. Eleven left us.

Friday, August 22, 1856, Florence, Nebraska, Martin Company, Samuel Openshaw Journal. We started at 8 o'clock and traveled about four miles when we arrived at the Missouri River, where we were ferried across to Florence. We went to the top of a hill where we could view the country all around, and the Missouri River to a great distance. Every place we came through, we were admired by the people very much. Some looked upon us as if we were deceived, others who were old apostates, came with all the subtlety of the devil, and all the cunning they have gained by their own experience, trying to turn the Saints to the right hand or to the left, but thanks be to God, few or none adhered to their advice.

Tuesday, September 9, 1856, Prairie Creek, Nebraska, Martin Company, John Jaques Journal. On the 9th of September, in the afternoon, the company came to a round pit or pond of water. Parched with thirst, the cattle rushed pell mell into the pond and stirred up the mud until the water was thick and black, before the people had supplied themselves for their own use. But it was all the water available, and so it was used for cooking purposes... [The meal] was quite black, but was eaten and drunk nevertheless. At 7 p.m. the camp started for Prairie Creek, nine miles, reaching it between 11 and 12 o'clock, but very glad to get to clear running water, after having been without two days.

Friday, September 12, 1856, Wood River, Nebraska, Martin Company, Samuel Openshaw Journal. Started about 8 o'clock; traveled about 4 miles when we came to the Wood River, which we crossed on a small bridge, continued down the side of it and stopped for dinner at 12 o'clock. For ought we knew ... a young man who walked with crutches had been left behind. We sent four men back to search for him, which caused us to move none today. About sunset, they brought him into the camp.

Thursday, October 9, 1856, Fort Laramie to the Last Crossing of the Platte, Martin Company, John Jaques Journal. Thurs. 9: Many of the brethren went to the fort to buy provisions, etc. I went and sold my watch for thirteen dollars. I bought from the fort commissariat 20 pounds of biscuit at 15 cents, twelve pounds of bacon at 15 cents and 3 pounds of rice at 17 cents and so on.

I believe the company left Fort Laramie the next day. Laramie Peak, in the distance, gave the first adequate idea of the Rocky Mountains--grand, gloomy and mysterious. Thenceforth, until the close of the journey we were so fully occupied in taking care of ourselves that we had little time to spare to note details with exactness, and many notes that were made at that time were lost. Up to this time the daily pound of flour ration had been regularly served out, but it was never enough to stay the stomachs of the emigrants, and the longer they were on the plains and in the mountains the hungrier they grew. It was an appetite that could not be satisfied. At least that was the experience of the handcart people. You felt as if you could almost eat a rusty nail or gnaw a file. You were ten times as hungry as a hunter, yea, as ten hunters, all the long day, and every time you woke up in the night. Eating was the grand passion of the pedestrian on the plains, an insatiable passion, for he never got enough to eat.

Near Fort Laramie one of the emigrants, after having eaten his supper one night, took a stroll through the camp of one of the wagon companies near by, where an acquaintance and friend kindly asked him to have some supper. With 'thanks' he thought he would. So he sat down with the wagon people and did full justice to some fried beef and bacon, with biscuit, which he thought was as savory a dish as he had tasted for many a day. After eating as long as he could put on a face to do so, he finished his second supper, but without feeling much more satisfied than when he first sat down. If anybody else had kindly extended to him another invitation to supper that night, I have no doubt he would have accepted gladly, and done full justice to the supper.

Well, at the time when the great appetite was fairly roused up and had put on its strength and was still further strengthened and sharpened by the increasing coldness of the weather, the extra pinching time commenced. Soon after Fort Laramie was passed, it was deemed advisable to curtail the rations in order to make them hold out as long as possible. The pound of flour fell to three-fourths of a pound, then to a half pound and subsequently lower. Still the company toiled on through the Black Hills, where the feed grew scarce for the animals also. As the necessities of man and beast increased, their daily food diminished.

The fourth pound of flour allotted each day was used by many people in the making of gruel. Mother Loader showed wisdom in making biscuits from the amount allotted to her family as bread was more substantial. When these were divided equally there remained one and one half biscuits. This she carried in her pocket and usually gave portions to her young son, Robert, when he became hungry. Once we came across a man who had fallen on the ground and was almost lifeless. She went to him and said, "Brother what is the matter, why do you not go on?" He replied, "Sister Loader, I cannot, I am too weak but if I had just one mouthful of bread I believe I could." She asked, "Do you think so and would you?" When he replied, "Yes," she took the bread from her pocket and gave it to him. After eating he arose and was again able to walk. When little Robert found that the bread was gone he said, "Mother you think more of that man than you do of me. You gave him my bread and, Oh!, I'm so hungry."

In the Black Hills the roads were harder, more rocky and more hilly, and this told upon the handcarts, causing them to fail more rapidly, become more rickety, and need more frequent repairing. One man's cart broke down one afternoon in the hills, and by some mischance the company all went on, leaving him behind, alone with the broken cart and his families little stock of worldly goods thereon, including his rations which he could not afford to leave. At this time he lost his knives and forks, and also some biscuits and butter and sugar which he had bought as extras at Laramie. He was drawing his little child in his cart as he had drawn her most of the journey, and as he subsequently drew her to the last crossing of the Platte, but when his cart broke down he had to transfer her to somebody else's cart and send her on with the company. So he remained behind with his cart, anxiously expecting somebody to turn back and help him, but no one came. Night drew on apace, and still he was all alone, save and excepting the presence of a prowling wolf, which could be seen in the streak of light on the western horizon, a little outside of ordinary rifle range. Happily, just as the darkness was settling down Captain Hunt's wagon company was observed coming down the opposite hill, from the east, at the base of which it encamped, a quarter of a mile distant from the benighted and lonely handcarter, who eagerly went and told his tale of misfortune to the wagon people, and they took him in for the night. Toward midnight two men with another cart from the handcart company, seven miles off, arrived in search of their missing companion. They also stayed with the wagon company that night, and the next morning early the three handcarters started after their own company, coming up with the camp just as it was breaking up and the emigrants were getting ready to start for the day's march.

Tuesday, October 14, 1856, along the North Platte River, Martin Company, John Jaques Journal. Traveled about 20 miles, baited [i.e., stopped for food, drink, and to feed livestock] about halfway, on the Platte River and camped on that river just after the road passes through a series of hills. Wagon company just before us all day. I was unwell today. My legs were swelled, also my hands, and I seemed very short of breath. Zilpah pulled the cart with me nearly all day.

Friday, October 17, 1856, near Deer Creek (along the North Platte River, east of Fort Casper), Martin Company, John Jaques Journal. Traveled about 5 miles and camped on Deer Creek. Washing done. Luggage reduced. Brother Scullthorpe being in advance stayed with Captain Hodgett's company. Owing to the growing weakness of emigrants and teams, the baggage including bedding and cooking utensils, was reduced to 10 pounds per head, children under 8 years, 5 pounds. Good blankets and other bedding and clothing were burned as they could not be carried further, though needed more badly than ever, for there was yet 400 miles of winter to go through.

Saturday, October 18, 1856, Fort Casper, Martin Company, Journal History. The company started at 9 o'clock a.m., traveled 15 miles and camped on the Platte River at 6 p.m., where the feed was tolerably good.

Saturday, October 18, 1856, Fort Casper, Martin Company, John Jaques Journal. Cool, fine day. Baited on creek. I was nearly half a mile behind. Made 17 miles. Camped on river. Good road before dinner, sandy and uneven after. Tamar at night took her rations with her mother. No cows killed tonight because the guard was reluctant to turn out.

Sunday, October 19, 1856, Last Crossing of the Platte near present-day Casper, Martin Company, John Jaques Journal. On the 19th of October the company crossed the Platte for the last time at Red Buttes, about 5 miles above the bridge.[19] That was a bitter cold day. Winter came on all at once, and that was the first day of it. The river was wide, the current strong, the water exceedingly cold and up to the wagon beds in the deepest parts, and the bed of the river was covered with cobble stones. Some of the men carried some of the women over on their backs or in their arms, but others of the women tied up their skirts and waded through, like heroines as they were, and as they had done through many other rivers and creeks. The company was barely over when snow, hail and sleet began to fall, accompanied by piercing north wind, and camp was made on this side of the river. An elderly man named Stone who was much weakened by diarrhea, went over the Platte bridge [Richard's Bridge] to

---

[19] Richard's Bridge.

avoid fording the river. He started up the northwest side of the river to meet and rejoin the company after it had crossed the ford, about five miles further up. Weary and weak, he may have sat down to rest on the way and have become benumbed with cold, or frozen to death. Be that as it may he was never seen again, but a portion of what was supposed to have been his body was afterwards found and brought into camp, having been ravaged by the wolves. Captain Hunt's wagon company camped on the other side of the river and Captain Hodgett's was on this side. That was a nipping night, and it told on the oxen as well as on the people.

Sunday, October 19, 1856, Last Crossing of the Platte, Martin Company, Patience Loader Account.[20] We

---

[20] The account of Patience Loader Rozsa Archer was written and included as part of the Journal of John Jaques. All references to the Patience Loader Account are from the John Jaques Journal. When Patience Loader's parents were baptized near Oxford, England in 1850, 23 year old Patience declined to join them because she liked fun and to her religion seemed "long-face." When she moved closer to home and witnessed the daily lives of the Latter-day Saints, she found their way of life attractive and was later baptized in June of 1853.

Along with her parents, three sisters and two brothers and in-laws, Patience emigrated to America in February 1856. The Loaders rented rooms in New York and planned to stay there for a year to earn enough money to outfit themselves for the westward trek. In May, however, they received word that they should leave immediately for Iowa City and prepare to travel west by handcart. James Loader died on the trail at the end of September, 1856, leaving Patience, her mother, her sisters and brothers to complete the trek by themselves. Her reminiscences were included with the Journal of John Jaques and begin just after the death of her father, and end with the Martin Company's entrance into the Salt Lake Valley on November 30. Patience died in 1921.

were in the Black Hills. We halted for a short time and took shelter under our carts. After the storm had passed we traveled on until we came to the last crossing of the Platte River. Here we met the wagon company. They were camped for the night. We of the handcart company had orders from Captain Martin to cross the river that afternoon and evening. As I said we had to cross the river. Mother went to see Sister Ballen in the Hunt wagon company and she gave Mother three good slices of bread and molasses for us girls. Mr. Parker from Centerville had been to England on a mission. After landing in New York he was taken very sick. Brother Weston took him to his home to take care of him. My sister, Maria, and myself took turns sitting up at night. He recovered his health sufficient to go home to Utah this season. He bought a mule and rode across the plains with the wagon company. When we met him at the Platte River he remembered our kindness to him. His heart went out in sympathy for mother and us girls when we told him that dear father was dead. He felt sorry to see us having to wade the river and pull the cart through. He took mother on his mule behind him, telling her to hold fast to him and he would return and bring the cart through the river. This we did not know he intended to do so we started to cross the river pulling our own cart. The water was deep and very cold and we were drifted out of the regular crossing and we came near to drowning. The water came up to our arm pits. Poor mother was standing on the bank screaming, as we got near the bank I heard her say, "For God's sake some of you men help my poor girls." Mother said she had been watching us and could see we were drifting down stream. Several of the brethren came down and pulled our cart up the bank for us and we got up the best way we could. Mother Loader showed great wisdom by carrying in her basket dry stockings to put on the family after they had waded streams, and on her body she wore extra underskirts for the same purpose. Mother took off her underskirts and apron and put on us to keep the wet clothing from us for we had to travel several miles before we could camp. Here mother took out from her apron the bread and molasses Sister Ballen gave her. She broke it into pieces and gave us each some. This was a great treat to us as we were all hungry. It seemed to give us new strength to travel.

When we were in the middle of the river I saw a poor man carrying his child on his back. He fell down in the water, I never knew if he was drowned or not. I felt sorry that we could not help him but we had all we could do to save ourselves from drowning.

We had to travel in our wet clothes until we got to camp. Our clothing was nearly frozen on us and when we got to camp we had very little dry clothing to put on. We had to make the best of our poor circumstances and put our trust in God that we take no harm. It was too late to go for wood and water. The wood was too far away. That night the ground was frozen so hard we were unable to drive any tent pins and the tent was wet. When we had taken it down in the morning it was somewhat frozen so we stretched it open the best we could and got in under it until morning. The bugle sounded early in the morning for we had to travel seven miles before we could get any wood to make a fire. We had many sick people, more than could ride in the sick wagon, so Captain Martin appointed Brother Ward to take charge of the invalids as he had traveled the plains so many times, having been on several missions. Brother Ward was started from camp long before the main company started. The poor man mistook the road and they were lost. It was a terrible day. It snowed and drifted and the wind blew all day. When we camped there was no sign of Brother Ward and his sick brethren. Captain Martin called for some of the brethren to go back and find the company of invalids. When it was getting dark they returned bringing nineteen, all chilled. I never knew if that was all that started out in the morning or not.

After we got to camp, we found we had to go a long way for wood. So, my sister, Maria, and myself went with the brethren to get the wood. We traveled in the snow knee deep for nearly a mile to the cedars. We found nothing but green cedar, as all the dry wood on the ground was covered with snow. I asked one of the brethren to cut me down a shoulder stick, so he kindly gave us quite a large, heavy log. My sister took one end on his shoulder and I raised the other end to my shoulder and we started back to camp. We had not gone far when we both fell down with our load. The deep snow made it very hard for us to get back to camp with the wood, but after much hard work we got there. My mother and sisters were anxiously waiting our return, for they were both hungry and cold. As soon as I could get some wood chopped, I tried to make a fire and cook a little broth, as I had an old beef's head. I was always on the lookout for anything I could get to eat, not only for myself but for the rest of the family. We removed the skin from the beefhead and chopped it up the best we could, put it into the pot with some snow and boiled it for a long time. About four o'clock in the afternoon we were able to have some broth. I cannot say that it tasted very good. It was flavored both with sage brush and smoke from our green cedar fire. But after it was cooked we felt very thankful to have that much. It would have tasted better if we had had a little pepper and salt, but that was a luxury we had been deprived of for a long time. This was our dinner and supper together. After we had eaten what we could the remainder was left for the next day. I put the fire in the bake oven and took it into the tent and we all sat around it to keep as warm as we could.

Sunday, October 19, 1856, Between the Last Crossing of the Platte and Red Buttes, Martin Company,

Heber R. McBride Journal.[21] We had to ford all the rivers but one and that was the Loupe Fork of the Platte but the evening we crossed the Platte for the last time it was very cold and the next morning there was about 6 inches of snow on the ground and then what we had to suffer can never be told. Father was very bad this morning--could hardly sit up in the tent we had to travel that day through the snow. I managed to get Father in to one of the wagons that morning and that was

---

[21]   Heber Robert McBride was born in Churchtown, England, May 13, 1843. He was 13 years old at the time of the handcart ordeal. After their family emigrated to America, they joined the Martin Handcart Company. There were 7 in the family. Heber was the oldest boy and he and his sister, who was 3 years older, had to pull their handcart all the way to Salt Lake. Their mother, who became very ill, would start out in the morning walking but before long she would give out and lay down and wait until her children came along and then they would put her on the cart and haul her until they came to camp for the evening.

Their father began to fail rapidly and after a while he could not pull the handcart any further. In Heber's Journal he records, "...there was 3 younger children than me and [one] so small she had to ride all the way for she was only about 3 years old the other 2 being boys managed to walk by holding on the handcart no tongue nor pen could tell what my Sister and me passed through our parents both sick and us young- it seemed as though death would be a blessing for we used to pray that we might die to get out of our misery..."

After arriving in Salt Lake City, Heber settled in Eden, in Ogden Valley. In 1865 he was called by Brigham Young to help rescue a group of immigrants stranded in the same general area where so many members of the 1856 handcart companies perished. In 1901 he moved to Alberta, Canada where he raised two families and passed away in 1925 at the age of 82. (This account was shared by and is used with permission of Ross Buckwalter, of Sandy, Utah, a grandson of Heber McBride.)

the last we ever saw of him alive we only made one drive as it began snowing very hard when we camped the snow was getting deep and my sister and me had to pitch our tent and get some wood but that was handy as there was plenty of dry willows on the bank of the river. After we had made Mother as comfortable as we could we went to try and find Father but the wind was blowing so bad that we could not see anything and the wagons had not got into camp and it was then after dark so we did not find him that night and the next morning the snow was about 18 inches deep and awful cold but while my sister was preparing our little bite of breakfast I went to look for Father and at last I found him under a wagon with snow all over him and he was stiff and dead. I felt as though my heart would burst--I sat down beside him on the snow and took hold of one of his hands and cried oh Father, Father. There we was away out on the Plains with hardly anything to eat and Father dead and mother sick and a widow with 5 small children and not able to live from day to another. After I had my cry out I went back to the tent and told Mother. Now to try and write to tell the feelings of Mother and the other children is out of the question. Now we were not all the family that was called upon to mourn the loss of a Father this morning for there was 13 men dead in camp. The men that was able to do anything cleaned [off] the snow and made a fire and thawed out the ground and dug a big hole and buried them in one grave some side by side and on top of one another-- any way to get them covered--for I can assure you that the men had no heart to do any more than they had to. We never knew how Father died whether he died in the wagon and was lifted out or he got out himself and fell down exhausted and froze to death. I don't know how many days we had to lay over for the snow was so deep that we could not pull our handcarts through and there we were in a starving condition and the oxen that pulled the wagons began dying but every one [the oxen] that died was devoured very quickly and us little boys would get strips of rawhide and try and eat it all. The [only] way they could do anything with it was to crisp it in the fire and then draw a string of it through our teeth and get some of the burnt scales of that way and then crisp it again and repeat the operation [till] we would get tired.

October, 1856, near the Last Crossing of the Platte, Martin Company, Patience Loader Account. We girls had drank our broth and mother was still drinking hers when the captain of the company and two other brethren fetched poor Brother Laurel to our tent. Since our father died, this brother had stayed in our tent as he had no friends with him. He was one of the invalids who was lost. Brother Stone said to mother, "Give him something warm." Mother said, "I have a little hot soup Patience made for us. I will share with him." We tried to give him a little soup with a teaspoon, but could not get the spoon between his teeth. Poor man, he looked at us, but could not speak a word. He was nearly frozen dead. We wrapped him up the best we could to try to get him warm, but he was too far gone. We all lay down on the frozen ground to try to get warm in our quilts. My mother, myself and sister Jane in one bed. Poor man, he had only one old blanket to wrap himself in and we had a burlap robe which we put over him. He commenced to talk to himself. He called for his wife and children. He had told me previously that he had a wife and nine children in London and that they would come out as soon as he could make enough money to send for them. In the night we could not hear him talking any more. I said to mother, "I think poor brother is dead. I have not heard him for the last hour." Mother asked me to get up and go to him. I got up but everything seemed so silent and dark and drear I said, "I cannot." She told me to get back in bed and keep warm and wait until daylight. Of course, we did not sleep. As soon as there was a little light I got up and went to the poor man and found him dead, frozen to the tent as I turned him over to look in his face. Never can I forget that sight. I told mother he was dead. She said to go tell Brother Toone. I went to his tent and told him. He told me to wrap him in a quilt and I said he had no quilts, only a small thin blanket and we could not spare any of our quilts as we had already used one to wrap my dear father in when he died. So we wrapped him in his own little blanket and the brethren came and took him away to bury him with eighteen more that died during the night. What a deplorable condition we were in at the time.

Sunday, October 19, 1856, Last Crossing of the Platte, Martin Company, Josiah Rogerson Account. Aaron Jackson was found so weak and exhausted when he came to the crossing of the Platte that he could not make it, and after he was carried across the ford in a wagon the writer was again detailed to wheel the dying Aaron on an empty cart, with his feet dangling over the end bar, to camp. After putting up his tent, I assisted his wife in laying him in his blankets. It was one of the bitter, cold, black frost nights, and notwithstanding the hard journey the day before, I was awakened at midnight to go on guard again till 6 or 7 in the morning. As I passed through the middle of the tent, my feet struck those of poor Aaron. They were stiff and rebounded at my accidental stumbling. Reaching my hand to his face, I found that he was dead, with his exhausted wife and little ones by his side, all sound asleep.... Returning to my tent from the night's guarding, I found there one of the most touching pictures of grief and bereavement in the annals of our journey. Mrs. Jackson was sitting by the side of her dead husband. Her face was suffused in tears, and between her bursts of grief and wails of sorrow, she would wring her hands and tear her hair. Her children blended their cries of "Father" with that of the mother. This was love, this was affection, grief of the heart, and bereavement of the soul, the like of which I have never seen since.

October, 1856, Red Buttes, Martin Company, Elizabeth Horrocks Jackson Kingsford.[22] About the 25th of Oct.[23], I think it was--I cannot remember the exact date-- we reached camp about sundown. My husband had for several days previous been much worse. He was still sinking, and his condition now became more serious. As soon as possible after reaching camp I prepared a little of such scant articles of food as we then had. He tried to eat but failed. He had not the strength to swallow. I put him to bed as quickly as I could. He seemed to rest easy and fell asleep. About nine o'clock I retired. Bedding had become very scarce, so I did not disrobe. I slept until, as it appeared to me, about midnight. I was extremely cold. The weather was bitter. I listened to hear if my husband breathed--he lay so still. I could not hear him. I became alarmed. I put my hand on his body, when to my horror I discovered that my worst fears were confirmed. My husband was dead. He was cold and stiff--rigid in the arms of death. It was a bitter freezing night and the elements had sealed up his mortal frame. I called for help to the other inmates of the tent. They could render me no aid; and there was no alternative but to remain alone by the side of the corpse till morning. The night was enveloped in almost Egyptian darkness. There was nothing with which to produce a light or kindle a fire. Of course I could not sleep. I could only watch, wait, and pray for dawn. But oh, how these dreary hours drew their tedious length along. When daylight came, some of the

---

[22] Entries by Elizabeth Horrocks Jackson Kingsford are from "Leaves from the Life of Elizabeth Horrocks Jackson Kingsford."

[23] Josiah Rogerson recalled these sad events as taking place on October 19.

male part of the company prepared the body for burial. And oh, such a burial and funeral service. They did not remove his clothing--he had but little. They wrapped him in a blanket and placed him in a pile with thirteen others who had died, and then covered him up in the snow. The ground was frozen so hard that they could not dig a grave. He was left there to sleep in peace until the trump of the Lord shall sound, and the dead in Christ shall awake and come forth in the morning of the first resurrection. We shall then again unite our hearts and lives, and eternity will furnish us with life forever more.

Monday, October 20, 1856, Red Buttes, Martin and Hunt Companies, Journal History. This morning the ground was covered with snow which prevented the company from moving. The cattle were driven into the corral in the afternoon, some 12 or 14 head being missing. It commenced snowing again at 3 p.m. and continued for some time.

October, 1856, Red Buttes, Martin Company, Elizabeth Horrocks Jackson Kingsford. It will be readily perceived that under such adverse circumstances I had become despondent. I was six or seven thousand miles from my native land, in a wild, rocky, mountain country, in a destitute condition, the ground covered with snow, the waters covered with ice, and I with three fatherless children with scarcely nothing to protect them from the merciless storms. When I retired to bed that night, being the 27th of Oct.,[24] I had a stunning revelation. In my dream, my husband stood by me and said, "Cheer up, Elizabeth, deliverance is at hand." The dream was fulfilled.

---

[24] By her account, this dream apparently took place two days after her husband died. If Josiah Rogerson's account is correct, this would mean that these events may have taken place on October 21.

Thursday, October 23, 1856, Red Buttes, Martin Company, John Jaques Journal. This next day after crossing the Platte, the company moved on slowly and camped again near the Platte at the point where the road left it for the Sweetwater. It snowed three days, and the teams and many of the people were so far given out that it was deemed advisable not to proceed further for a few days, but rather to stay in camp and recruit. It was hoped that the snow and cold would prove only a foretaste of winter and would soon pass away and the weather would moderate, but that hope proved elusive. In this camp the company stayed, resting and recruiting as well as could be under the circumstances, the snow remaining on the ground and the frost being very keen at nights. Here the flour fell to four ounces per day. In addition to the flour ration, considerable beef was killed and served to the company, as had been the case most of the journey. But the cattle had now grown so poor that there was little flesh left on them, and that little was as lean as could be. The problem was how to cook it to advantage. Stewed meat and soups were found to be bad for diarrhea and dysentery, provocative of and aggravating those diseases, of which there was considerable in the company, and to fry lean meat without an atom of fat in it or out of it was disgusting to every cook in camp. The outlook was certainly not encouraging, but it need not be supposed that the company was in despair, notwithstanding the situation was rather desperate. Oh! No! A hopeful and cheerful spirit pervaded the camp, and the "Songs of Zion" were frequently heard at this time, though the company was in the very depths of privation. Though the bodies of the people were worn down, their spirits were buoyant, while at the same time they had become so accustomed to looking death in the face that they seemed to have no fear of it.

Thursday, October 23, 1856, Red Buttes, Martin Company, Journal History. The weather was very cold and frosty. William Upton who arrived from Capt. Hodgett's company the previous evening by Jesse Haven to consult Dr. Wiseman, died of mortification at the heart aged 34 years. The camp was still detained because of snow. By this time several of the cattle had died.

Tuesday, October 28, 1856, Red Buttes, Martin Company, Church Chronology--Andrew Jenson. Capt. Edward Martin's handcart company, detained by the unusual early snowstorms of the season, was met by Joseph Young, Daniel W. Jones and Abel Garr, at a point sixteen miles above the Platte bridge. Three days later [October 31] the company arrived at Greasewood Creek, where four wagons of the relief company, in charge of Geo. D. Grant, loaded with provisions and some clothing for the suffering emigrants were awaiting them.

Tuesday, October 28, 1856, Red Buttes, Martin Company, John Jaques Journal.[25] The 28th of October was the red letter day to this handcart expedition. On that memorable day Joseph A. Young, Daniel W. Jones and Abel Garr galloped unexpectedly into camp amid the cheers and tears and smiles and laughter of the emigrants. Those three men, being the most advanced relief company from Salt Lake, brought the glad word that assistance, provisions, and clothing were near, that ten wagons were waiting at Devil's Gate for the emigrants, which cheering intelligence had been previously communicated to Captain Hodgett's wagon company, in camp hard by, and first reached by the express, who after a very brief stay in the handcart company pushed on to Captain Hunt's

---

[25] See also Journal History, 30 Nov 1856, p.22.

wagon company, encamped on the Platte beyond the handcart company. The express stayed with Hunt's company for the night. All was now animation and bustle in the handcart camp, everybody was busy at once in making preparations for a renewed start in the morning. The revived spirits of the company were still exhilarated by an increased ration of flour that day.

Tuesday, October 28, 1856, Red Buttes, Martin Company, Patience Loader Account. They came to our fire seeking us out there. Brother Young asked, "How many are dead and how many are still living?" I told him I did not know. With tears streaming down his face he asked, "Where is your Captain's tent?" He called for the bugler to call everyone out of their tents. Then he told Captain Martin if he had flour enough to give us all one pound of flour each and said if there were any cattle to kill, to give us one pound of beef each, saying there were plenty of provisions and clothing coming for us on the road, but tomorrow we must make a move from here. He said we would have to travel twenty-five miles then there would be plenty of provisions and there would be good brethren to help us, that they had come with good teams and covered wagons so the sick could ride. Then he said he would have to leave us. He would like to have traveled with us the next morning, but we must cheer up and God would bless us and give us strength. He said, "We have made a trail for you to follow." These brethren had to go still further, to the Platte River as the Hunt wagon company was stilled camped there and they were in great distress as their teams had given out and so many provisions were giving out.

After the brethren had left us, we felt quite encouraged and we got our flour and beef before night came on and we were all busy cooking and we felt to thank God and our kind brethren that had come to help us in our great distress and misery for we were suffering greatly with cold and hunger.

When night came we went to bed. We slept pretty comfortably more so than we had done for some time. We felt assured.

Wednesday, October 29, 1856, Avenue of Rocks, Martin Company, John Jaques Journal. Early on the morning of the 29th the handcart company [left the North Platte at Red Buttes and] struck across country for the Sweetwater. Joseph A. Young and his companions, returning from Hunt's company, overtook Martin's company before night and camped with us at Rocky Avenue, about thirty [36] miles east of Devil's Gate.[26]

Wednesday, October 29, 1856, Avenue of Rocks, Martin Company, Patience Loader Account. We were all glad to move from this place. It seemed that if God our Father had not sent help to us that we must all have perished and died in a short time, for at that time we had only very little provisions left and at the request of Captain Martin we had come on four ounces of flour a day for each one to make the flour last as long as we could. I don't know how long we could have lived and pulled our handcarts on this small quantity of food. Our provisions would not have lasted as long as they did had all our company lived, but many of them died causing our provisions to hold out longer. I remember well poor Brother Blair. He was a fine, tall man, had been one of Queen Victoria's life guards in London. He had a wife and four children. He made a cover for his cart and put his four children on the cart. He pulled his cart alone, his wife helped by pushing behind. The poor man was so weak and worn down that he fell several times that day but still he kept his dear little children on the cart all day. This man had so much love for

---

[26] The insertions in this entry appear in the Journal History, from November 30, 1856.

his wife and children that instead of eating his morsel of food himself he would give it to his children. Poor man, he pulled the cart as long as he could, then he died and his wife and children had to do the best they could without his help. The children got frozen. Some parts of their bodies were all sores, but they got to Salt Lake City alive.

There was poor William Whittaker. He was in the tent with several others. He and his brother, John, occupied one part of a tent. In the other part another family was sleeping. There was a young woman sleeping and she was awakened by poor Brother Whittaker eating her fingers. He was dying with hunger and cold. He also ate the flesh of his own fingers that night. He died and was buried at Willow Springs before we left camp that morning.

Friday, October 31, 1856, Greasewood [Horse] Creek, Martin Company, John Jaques Journal. Fri. 31: Windy morning. Fine afternoon. Baited about 5 miles. Afternoon met Elder C.H. Wheelock, Daniel W. Jones and David Garr[27] coming to meet the companies. Elder Wheelock said that he thought of sending me to Captain Hunt's wagon company. About dark arrived at Greasewood Creek [between 30 and 40 miles from the Last Crossing of the Platte], where we found Elders G.D. Grant, Charles Decker, C.G.Webb, R.T. Burton and other Brethren from the valley with six wagons laden with flour and other things, who had come to the assistance of the belated emigrants. This was a time of joy. Several of the brethren came a mile or two to meet us and helped to pull some of the carts. Here some stockings, boots and other clothing were distributed among the emigrants, also a few onions, which were highly prized, and a pound of flour

---

[27] Other accounts make it probable this reference should be to David's brother, Abel Garr.

ration was served out. This was the beginning of better days as to food and assistance, but the cold grew more severe and was intense much of the way.

The snow began to fall very fast and continued until late at night. You can imagine between 500 and 600 men, women and children, worn down by drawing handcarts through snow and mud, fainting by the wayside, falling chilled by the cold; children crying, their limbs stiffened by the cold, their feet bleeding, and some of them bare to snow and frost. The sight is almost too much for the stoutest of us. Our company is too small to help much. It is only a drop in a bucket, as it were in comparison with what is needed. I think not over one third of Martin's company is able to walk. This you may think is extravagant, but it is nevertheless true. Some of them have good courage and are in good spirits, but a great many are like little children, and do not help themselves much more, nor realize what is before them. Brother Charles Decker has now traveled this road the forty-ninth time, and he says he has never before seen so much snow on the Sweetwater at any season of the year. Brother Hunt's company are two or three days behind us, yet Brother Wheelock will be with them to counsel them, also some of the other brethren who came out.

Friday, October 31, 1856, Greasewood [Horse] Creek, Martin Company, Patience Loader Account. It was a nice, bright morning but very cold and clear. The snow was very deep in places. It was hard pulling the cart, I will say that we traveled on all day in the snow, but the weather was fine and in the middle of the day the sun was quite warm. Some time in the afternoon a strange man appeared to me as we were resting. He came and looked in my face. He said, "Are you Patience?" I said, "Yes." He said, "I thought it was you. Travel on, there is help for you. You will come to a good place. There is plenty." With this he was gone. He disappeared. I looked but never saw where he went. This seemed very strange to me. I took this as some one sent to encourage us and give us strength. We traveled on and got into camp. There were five or six brethren with their wagons camped there. They had been and got quantities of wood and they had already made a dozen big fires for us and there was plenty of lovely water. That was a great treat to us for we had had nothing but snow water and that did not taste good as we had to melt it over the camp fire. It tasted of sage brush, and sometimes of cedar wood smoke. We felt very thankful to our brethren for making us these good fires and supplying us with wood so abundantly. I really must say I was very thankful, for since our dear father died, it had fallen on me and my sister, Maria, to get most of our wood and I thought it was good that we did not have wood to get that night after such hard pulling all day through the snow. It was nearly dark when we got to camp. It seemed good to get a pound of flour again that night. The brethren fetched out some provisions and clothing. I was thankful to get a nice warm quilted hood, which was very warm and comfortable. I also got a pair of slippers as I was nearly barefoot. We still had to pull our handcarts as there was not wagons sufficient for us to ride. Only those that were sick could ride. A brother from the valley came to our camp. He asked if I knew of a certain family. I told the brother that there were the two children living in this company, but that the father had become discouraged and stayed at Laramie and that the mother had died. At this the poor man broke down and said, "She was my poor dear sister. As soon as I heard of the trouble and distress of this handcart company, I made ready to come in search of my sister and family. Where are the children?" I directed him to the wagon they were in as he wanted to take them into his wagon. He said he had fetched provisions and a feather bed and good warm blankets and quilts for his sister. I told this brother how these two poor boys had suffered severely with cold and hunger since their poor mother had died. One morning as we were getting ready to leave

69

camp, I saw these dear boys, one eleven and the other not more than four or five years old. The older boy was crawling along on his hands and knees. His poor feet were so frozen the blood ran from them into the snow as the poor thing made his way along to the sick wagon. The other poor dear child was crying by his brother's side, and his poor little arms and hands all covered with sores from chilblains, and scarcely anything on to cover his poor little body. Many years later I heard that they were still living and doing well.

Hunt and Hodgett Wagon Companies, 1856

September 1856, along the Platte River, Hunt Wagon Company, Mary Goble Pay.[28] The family of Mary Goble Pay "was converted in Brighton, England, in 1856. They sold their possessions and sailed from Liverpool with 900 others on the vessel Horizon. After six weeks at sea they landed at Boston and then traveled by steam train to Iowa City for fitting out. There they purchased two yoke of oxen, one yoke of cows, a wagon, and a tent. They were assigned to travel with and assist one of the handcart companies.

"At Iowa City their first tragedy also occurred. Their youngest child, less than two years of age, suffering from exposure, died and was buried in a grave never again visited by a member of the family."

The following account was written by Mary Goble Pay, who is the grandmother of Sister Marjorie Pay Hinckley, and was thirteen years old at the time of these experiences: "We traveled from fifteen to twenty-five miles a day... till we got to the Platte River.... We caught up with the handcart companies that day. We watched them cross the river. There

---

[28] As quoted by President Gordon B. Hinckley, Ensign, July 1984, p.6.

were great lumps of ice floating down the river. It was bitter cold. The next morning there were fourteen dead.... We went back to camp and had our prayers and... sang 'Come, Come Ye Saints, No Toil Nor Labor Fear.' I wondered what made my mother cry that night.... The next morning my little sister was born.... We named her Edith. She lived six weeks and died.... She was buried at the last crossing of the Sweetwater."

Wednesday, September 24, 1856, along the Platte River, Hunt Company, Journal History. Sister Mary Goble, wife of William Goble of Brighton, England, was delivered of a daughter in the morning. The company started at 9 o'clock a.m., traveled until sundown and camped for the night after making a distance of 14 miles. During the day, the company traveled over a sandy road. The feed at this place was good.

Thursday, October 3, 1856, along the Platte River, Hunt Company, Journal History. The company resumed the journey at 9 o'clock a.m., the weather being fine, but the roads heavy, leading over high hills and wet, sandy ground. After traveling 7 miles, the company went into camp at 2 p.m., near the Platte River, where the feed was scarce. Margaret Price, wife of John Price of Pembrokeshire, Wales, was delivered of a daughter.

October 1856, Red Buttes, Hodgett Company, John Bond Journal.[29] *John Bond, a twelve-year old boy when he crossed the plains with the Hodgett Wagon Company, wrote the following:* "The bugle is sounded again by John Wadkins to call all the Saints together for prayers to ask the infinite Father to bring food, medicines, and other things necessary for the

---

[29] John Bond, Handcart West in '56, p. 23. This Journal is in the possession of the Utah State Historical Society.

sick and needy. After prayers, all are ordered to bed. I [had seen someone prepare] a nice pot of dumplings just before the bugle sounded. She hid the dumplings under the wagon, being a zealous woman, and went to prayer meeting, but I did not go this time. I stood back and looked for the dumplings, found them and being so hungry I could not resist the temptations, sat down and ate them all. I admit that those dumplings did me more good than all the prayers that could have been offered but I felt I had done a great wrong in that act and I regret it and ask God to forgive me for that temptation that overcame [me] in a time of hunger."

Sunday, November 2, 1856, East of Willow Springs, Hunt Company, Journal History. During the night, a hard frost had prevailed and several of the cattle had strayed away. Search was made for some distance around the camp but they could not be found. Those who had their teams traveled on to Willow Springs, from which place oxen were sent back to bring up the other wagons afterwards. Capts. John A. Hunt and Gilbert Spencer went back to the previous day's camping place and found the missing oxen, which they brought to camp late in the evening. At this place, the snow was 6 or 7 inches deep, and the weather was very cold. The brethren cut down willows for the oxen. The company had traveled 4 miles during the day. A meeting was held in the camp in the evening addressed by Elders Wheelock, Webb and Broomhead, and a unanimous vote was taken that all the emigrating Saints would be willing to do as they were instructed, even if it was required of them to leave all they had behind and be glad to get into the Valley with their lives only. They agreed to cease complaining at coming so late in the season, as everything was being done to start the company.

Monday, November 3, 1856, Greasewood [Horse] Creek, Hunt Company, Journal History. The company started at 10:30 a.m., the weather being very cold. Fourteen or fifteen oxen were left on the road. The night encampment was formed on Greasewood Creek, half a mile from the crossing, at 8 p.m., after traveling 11 miles, during the day. The infant child of William Goble died at 9 o'clock p.m. From this date on, the camp journal was written with lead pencil which at this late day, February 25, 1926, can scarcely be read. It would appear that the ink used by the scribe had frozen, and the journal from now on only contained a few entries.

CHAPTER 2
THE TRAIL TO MARTIN'S COVE

Just west of Independence Rock, the Sweetwater River flows through a high gorge with 400' cliffs on each side. The gorge is called **Devil's Gate.** There is no room to travel next to the river, so the trail goes around the south side of the mountain. Because of the unique beauty of the place, many travelers would hike and climb up the ridge to look down at the river rushing through the gorge. Some slipped and fell to their deaths, including an 18 year old woman who died there in the early 1860's. The epitaph on her graveboard said: "Here lies the body of Caroline Todd; Whose soul has lately gone to God; Ere redemption was too late; She was reclaimed at Devil's Gate."

The area around Devil's Gate today is known as part of the **Sun Ranch.** It was first settled by Tom Sun in 1872, and remained in the Sun family for many generations. Tom Sun was a true frontiersman, trapper, and Indian Scout. He was a friend of Buffalo Bill, and used this part of the ranch as a favorite site for his hunting parties.

Just west of Devil's Gate is a spot that has come to be called **Martin's Cove.** It has become symbolic of the terrible cost in human life paid by the Willie and Martin handcart companies of 1856. "A monument erected by the Utah Pioneer Trails & Landmarks Association, and citizens of Wyoming, June 22, 1933, stands on the north shoulder of abandoned highway State 220 at a point 2.0 miles west of the Sun Ranch. It states: 'Survivors of Captain Edward Martin's handcart company of Mormon emigrants from England to Utah were rescued here in perishing condition about Nov. 12, 1856. Delayed in starting and hampered by inferior carts, it was

74

overtaken by an early winter. Among the company of 576, including aged people and children, the fatalities numbered 145. Insufficient food and clothing and severe weather caused many deaths. Toward the end every campground became a graveyard. Some of the survivors found shelter in a stockade and mail station near Devil's Gate where their property was stored for the winter. Earlier companies reached Utah safely.'"[30]

In August, 1992, President Hinckley dedicated a monument at Martin's Cove. The Church News reported: "The 'second rescue' of the Willie and Martin handcart pioneers is nearing completion, 136 years after the starving pioneers were rescued in the midst of freezing blizzards on the high plains of Wyoming.

"The first rescue in the late fall of 1856 involved men and wagons, loaded with food, clothing and other provisions, sent by Brigham Young. He had received word from returning missionaries that the two handcart companies and the Hunt and Hodgett wagon companies backing them up were destitute and in danger of perishing from exposure and hunger.

"The second rescue by leaders and members of the Riverton Wyoming Stake, through which the Mormon Pioneer Trail crosses for many miles in central Wyoming, is not for temporal welfare but for eternal salvation. The rescue is to ensure that the temple work for all the Willie and Martin handcart pioneers has been or will be completed.

President Hinckley on Aug. 15, 1992, traveled more than 200 miles through desolate, sagebrush country--about 45 miles of the trip was over rough, rocky dirt roads--to dedicate three monuments in two separate ceremonies. The monuments identify two sites where the handcart pioneers were rescued,

---

[30] Haines, 1972.

and another site marks Rocky Ridge, the highest point on the Mormon Trail. Because of its high altitude and rugged terrain, Rocky Ridge is thought to be one of the most difficult portions of the entire trail -- a trail described by President Hinckley as 'a trail of tragedy, a trail of faith, a trail of devotion, a trail of consecration, even the consecration of life itself.'

"At the monument site on the sagebrush hill, swept by the Wyoming winds, President Hinckley, who was accompanied by his wife, Marjorie, the Riverton stake presidency; and a small group of others, said in his dedicatory prayer: 'Terrible was the suffering of those who came here to find some protection from the heavy storms of that early winter. With their people hungry, cold and dying from sheer exhaustion, they came up into this cove for shelter. And then they died here, some 56 people. They are buried somewhere in this earth. We stand here with bare heads and grateful hearts for their sacrifices, and the sacrifices of all who were with them along this tragic trail.'

"He dedicated the monument 'as a memorial to those faithful and wonderful people.... who gave of their lives in many instances, and certainly gave of their strength in an exercise of faith [that] finally led them to their place in the valley, aided by good and valiant and wonderful men, who, at the peril of their own lives, came to rescue them here.'

"President Hinckley prayed that the site may be visited by 'generations yet to come, who, like we, may bow their heads in reverent remembrance of our forebears who paid so costly a price for the faith which they carried in their hearts.'"[31]

---

[31] Church News, Aug 22, 1992.

1847 Pioneer Company

Monday, June 21, 1847, Devil's Gate, Pioneer Company, William Clayton. President Young, Kimball and others went to view the north side of Devil's Gate and returning reported that the Devils would not let them pass, or meaning that it was impossible to go through the Gateway, so called. We proceeded on a little further and at 25 minutes to 7 formed our encampment on the bank of the river having traveled this afternoon 7 3/4 miles and during the day 15 1/4. The feed here is good and plentiful and a little Cedar can be obtained at the foot of one of the rocky ridges about a quarter of a mile back for fuel. After we had camped I went back to view the "Devil's Gate" where the river runs between two high rocky ridges for the distance of about 200 yards. The rock on the east side is perpendicular and was found by a Barometrical measurement by Elder Pratt to be 399 feet 4 1/2 inches high.

Tuesday, June 22, 1847, near Devil's Gate, Pioneer Company, Heber C. Kimball. After we had camped I walked on the high bluff with Elder Woodruff. We found it steep and hard labor to get up. When we arrived at the top, we could see very little farther than when on the level on account of the mountains. We, however, kneeled down together and offered up our prayers for the Camp, the Saints, and especially our dear families.

Willie Handcart Company, 1856

Wednesday, October 15, 1856, Devil's Gate, Willie Company, William Woodward, Clerk. Early this morning, Caroline Reeder from Linstead, Suffolk, England, aged 17 years, died. The camp rolled on passed 'Devil's Gate' & nooned after traveling about 6 miles. The camp rolled on & we camped on the banks of the Sweetwater after making about

16 miles travel thro' the day. Many of the company are sick & have to ride in the wagons. One beef heifer & one poor cow were killed this evening for the camp. Last evening a council and a meeting were held to take into consideration our provisions & the time it was considered we should have to make it last before we could depend upon supplies. It was unanimously agreed to reduce the rations of flour one fourth-- the men then would get 10 1/2 ozs. per day; women & large children 9 ozs. per day; children 6 ozs. per day; & infants 3 ozs. per day each.

Wednesday, October 15, 1856, Devil's Gate, Willie Company, Levi Savage Journal. Sweetwater. Today we traveled fifteen and a half miles. Last night Caroline Reeder, aged seventeen years, died and was buried this morning. The people are getting weak and failing very fast. A great many are sick. Our teams are also failing fast, and it requires great exertion to make any progress. Our rations were reduced last night, one quarter, bringing the men to ten ounces and the women to nine ounces. Some of the children were reduced to six and others to three ounces each.

Wednesday, October 15, 1856, Devil's Gate, Willie Company, David Reeder Family History. On October 15th, your sister, Caroline, left the camp one evening to hunt for wood--she was chilled through and through. As she did not return, I went in search and found her crouched down behind a bush. But I was too late. She was departed. All we could do was to lay her tenderly away as best we could.

The Rescue Party, 1856

To better understand the story of the Martin Company, and their ordeal at Martin's Cove, one must look west several weeks before their arrival at the site. The Utah Saints responded quickly when they heard of the distress of the handcart Saints. The following entries explain the formation of the rescue party and some of the rescuers' movements east from Salt Lake City.

Friday, September 26, 1856, Salt Lake City, First Two 1856 Handcart Companies Arrive, Church Chronology--Andrew Jenson. The first two companies of immigrating Saints, which crossed the plains with handcarts, arrived at G.S.L. City, in charge of Edmund Ellsworth and Daniel McArthur. They were welcomed by the First Presidency of the Church, a brass band, a company of lancers and a large concourse of citizens.

Saturday, October 4, 1856, Salt Lake City, Missionaries Arrive, Church Chronology--Andrew Jenson. Apostle Franklin D. Richards, Daniel Spencer, ... and a number of other missionaries, arrived in G.S.L. City.

Saturday, October 4, 1856, Salt Lake City, Journal History. The Presidency with returned missionaries and some others met in the Historian's Office to Council about sending back provisions, teams, etc. to meet the P.E. Fund Immigration.... Pres. Brigham Young said the object of my meeting the brethren here is to find out what we need to do tomorrow. It is the day for calling upon the bishops.

Sunday, October 5, 1856, Salt Lake City, General Conference, Church Chronology--Andrew Jenson. The General semi-annual conference of the church was commenced in G.S.L. City. It continued three days.

Sunday, October 5, 1856, Salt Lake City, General Conference, Journal History, Comments of Brigham Young. I feel disposed to be as speedy as possible in our operations

79

with regard to helping our brethren who are now on the plains, consequently I shall call upon the people forthwith for the help that is needed. I want them to give their names this morning, if they are ready to start on their journey tomorrow morning and not say, "I will go next week or in ten days or in a fortnight hence," for I wish you to start tomorrow morning.

I want the sisters to have the privilege of fetching blankets, skirts, stockings, shoes, etc. for the men, women and children that are in those handcart companies.....

I request the elders of Israel who have been on missions abroad, also those that are now on missions, to keep the spirit of their missions, if they have to; do not lay off your gospel armor.... I said to my son Joseph this morning, mingle not with those that you associated with previous to going on your mission, unless they will follow you instead of your following them.... Our elders have got to take a stand to never follow the crowd, but to walk in the footsteps of their Redeemer... keep your armor bright,...for your spiritual labors are wanted in this city and Territory more than they are in England....

I tell you that the person that keeps his eye upon the mark never considers what he passes through, never thinks about it, whether it be in walking and pulling handcarts, or traveling on foot, going without food and shelter, wandering to and fro, to labor for the people. Saints never think of what they suffer or pass through, it never comes into their minds....

The Lord has blessings for the people; they might have angels visit, if their lives had been according to their profession; and the power of the Lord would have defended this people. But no, we must be driven from city to city, and hunted from land to land; why? Because we did not live our religion; that is the only reason....

If you ask me whether the time will ever come when you may have the privilege of laying off your armor and ceasing that watchful care that we have now to keep; not before...all Israel [is] gathered and saved; not before the wicked are thrust out, and Jesus Christ comes to take charge of the Church on earth…. Until then we shall have to keep our armor on, and, figuratively speaking, fight with sword in hand against our enemies all the time.

Sunday, October 5, 1856, Salt Lake City, General Conference, Journal History, Comments of Wilford Woodruff. When I saw Br. Ellsworth come into this city covered with dust and drawing a handcart, I felt that he had gained greater honor than the riches of this world could bestow and he looked better to me than he would have done had he been clothed with the most costly apparel that human ingenuity can produce; he looked better I say than a man adorned with jewels and finery of every description. The honor any man can obtain by his faithfulness in this cause and kingdom is worth far more than all the honors of the world.

Sunday, October 5, 1856, Salt Lake City, General Conference, Daniel W. Jones Account.[32] Brother Young

---

[32] This is not the Captain Dan Jones from Wales who was also in Carthage Jail with the Prophet Joseph prior to his Martyrdom. A brief description might be helpful in describing this Dan Jones who joined the rescue effort.

In 1847 Daniel W. Jones enlisted with the Missouri volunteers for service in the war with Mexico. After the war he remained in Mexico until 1850, when he returned to Santa Fe. There he joined a group of frontiersmen in the task of driving 8,000 sheep via Salt Lake Valley to Upper California.

After a near fatal accident on the Green River, he was left by his companions in a Mormon Settlement on the Provo River near Utah Lake. "On arriving at the [settlement]… [I] was determined that I would stay and see for myself, and if Mormonism was what they said it was, I would go no further for all the gold in California. Since I was ten years old I had believed there was something before called upon every one present to lend a hand in fitting up these teams. As I was going out with the crowd, Brother Wells spoke to me saying: "You are a good hand for the trip; get ready." Soon after Bishop Hunter said the same thing to me. Also Brother Grant met me and said: "I want you on this trip." I began to think it time to decide, so I answered, "All right." I had a saddle horse. We were instructed to get everything we could ready and rendezvous between the Big Mountain and Little Mountains, a short day's drive out from Salt Lake.

Monday, October 6, 1856, Salt Lake City, General Conference, Wilford Woodruff Journal. Conference met at the Bowery this morning at 10 o'clock.... After singing and prayer President Young said our conference is now open and the first business is to gather together the clothing sh[oes?] flour and Teams and men and start them, into the mountains after the Hand Cart & other Companies who are back on the plains. [He then lists quite a few articles.] This offering was made By request of President Brigham Young for the poor.

President Kimball moved that President Young and Himself and J.M. Grant Should go into the mountains to Meet the companies and bring them out. The vote was put to the people but few voted for but the great majority against it.

---

me worth living for and that God would eventually answer my prayers and let me know how to serve him."

After casting a curious eye about him at the Mormons, he took kindly toward them and on January 27th, 1851, he was baptized. The remainder of his adventurous lifetime was spent as peacemaker to the warring Indian tribes, missionary to the Indians, and frontier scout. For more information about the life of Daniel W. Jones, refer to Forty Years Among the Indians.

Tuesday, October 7, 1856, Salt Lake City, The First Rescue Party, Journal History, R.T. Burton Account. Left G.S.L. City, going east, to meet the emigrating companies. Camped tonight at the foot of the Big Mountain.

Tuesday, October 7, 1856, Salt Lake City, The First Rescue Party, Journal of Redick Newton Allred. I responded to a call upon the brethren to assist them... and on the 7th about 50 men and 20 four-horse wagons with 10 ton of flour with other provisions and clothing left the city. I got a pony to ride from William B Pace. George D. Grant camped at the foot of the big mountain with 10 wagons and I camped at the east foot of the little mountain with 10 wagons.

Tuesday, October 7, 1856, Salt Lake City, The First Rescue Party, Daniel W. Jones Account. Next day teams and volunteers were ready. A better outfit and one more adapted to the work before us I do not think could have possibly been selected if a week had been spent in fitting up. Besides the wagons and teams, several men went horseback. We had good teams and provisions in abundance. But best of all, those going were alive to the work and were of the best material possible for the occasion.

Tuesday, October 14, 1856, Black's Fork of the Green River, Wyoming, The First Rescue Party, R.T. Burton Account. Brother Smoot returned with us to meet his son, camped tonight on Black's Fork. Again sent on an express to meet the company and report back to us their situation, whereabouts, etc. [They agreed that the express would wait at Devil's Gate if they did not find the Martin Company before then, according to Woodruff's journal entry on November 13.] The express was carried by Cyrus H. Wheelock, Joseph A. Young, Steven Taylor, and Abel Garr."

Sunday, October 19, 1856, South Pass, The First Rescue Party, Harvey Cluff Account.[33] When they crossed the Continental Divide at South Pass, a storm met them head-on. From that time on they encountered increasingly cold days and bitter nights. When an animal was killed to take to the immigrants, there was no need to salt the beef--it froze during quartering and stayed frozen. It now seemed necessary to leave more teams behind so that they might be able to assist when the immigrant parties came through. Therefore, Redick Allred was stationed on the Sweetwater River with flour, cattle, eleven guards, and four wagons. He would soon be joined from the west by three additional wagons and six men. Had anyone in the relief party foreseen the condition of either of the handcart companies, they would have gathered all the stores and teams at Fort Bridger, Green River, and South Pass and traveled day and night until their animals broke. It was just as well they did not know, for the relief effort would already require more strength and supplies then they carried. Their pace would already stretch every man to the breaking point. Captain Burton had seen rigorous action in Tooele County while chasing Indian marauders; his company had been caught in summer with no water and in winter with no tents, bedding, or warm coats. But of the present campaign he would later state, "This was the hardest trip of my life."

Sunday, October 19, 1856, Willow Creek, The First Rescue Party, Journal of Redick Newton Allred. The 19th, Captain Grant left me in charge of the supplies of flour, beef cattle, 4 wagons, the weak animals and 11 men for guard. I killed the beef cattle and left the meat lay in quarters where it

---

[33] Just to give an indication of the age of most of the rescuers, Harvey Cluff was 20 years old. Another member of the rescue party, David Kimball, son of Heber C. and Vilate Kimball, was only 18 years old.

froze and kept well as it was very cold and storming almost every day. We were reinforced by 3 wagons and 6 men loaded with flour.

Monday, October 20, 1856, Rock Creek, The First Rescue Party, Harvey Cluff Account. For protection of ourselves and animals, the company moved down the river to where the willows were dense enough to make a good protection against the raging storm from the north. The express team had been dispatched ahead as rapidly as possible to reach and give encouragement to the faltering emigrants, by letting them know that help was near at hand. Quietly resting in the seclusion of the willow copse, three miles from the road I volunteered to take a sign board and place it at a conspicuous place at the main road. This was designed to direct the express party who were expected to return about this time. So they would not miss us. In facing the northern blast up hill I found it quite difficult to keep from freezing. I had only been back to camp a short time when two men rode up from Willie's handcart company. The signboard had done the work of salvation. Had Captain Willie and his fellow traveller, from his company, continued on the road they certainly would have perished as they would have reached the Sweetwater where the storm first struck us. The handcart company was then 25 miles from our camp [this is a 2 mile difference from Broomhead's account], and as they had traveled that distance without food for themselves or horses and no bedding, they must have perished. I have always regarded this act of mine as the means of their salvation. And why not? An act of that importance is worthy of record and hence I give a place here.

Sunday, October 26, 1856, Devil's Gate, The First Rescue Party, R.T. Burton Account. Traveled 19 miles; camped near Devil's Gate; found the express that had been sent on at this place, waiting further orders. Had heard nothing from the company behind [Martin Company].

Sunday, October 26, 1856, Devil's Gate, The First Rescue Party, William Broomhead Diary. Fine morning. All is well. Travelled within 2 miles of the Devil's Gate and camped. Express was at the gate, had been there 4 days and had heard nothing of the carts. They came up to our camp, singing after supper, prayer by J. Young.

Sunday, October 26, 1856, Devil's Gate, The First Rescue Party, Harvey Cluff Account. On arriving at Devil's Gate we found the expressmen awaiting our coming up, for as yet they had no word as to where the companies were. Here we were in a dilemma. Four or five hundred miles from Salt Lake and a thousand emigrants with handcarts on the dreary plains and the severity of winter already upon us.... Devil's Gate is formed by the Sweetwater river cut through a mountain of granite rock 1000 feet in length 130 feet wide with perpendicular walls of 400 feet in height. Irregular ranges of low hills or mountains dot the irregular plains. The hills are covered sparsely with cedars and scrubby pitch pine timber. The plains were pasture for buffalo, deer and antelope, but those animals, except an occasional antelope, had gone to other parts. Devil's Gate consisted of a small stockade and a few log houses, located on a plain near where the river enters the deep gorge through the mountains.

Monday, October 27, 1856, Devil's Gate, The First Rescue Party, R.T. Burton Account. Remained in the same place. Feed tolerably good. From this point sent another express to the bridge [Richard's Bridge] on Platte River, Joseph A. Young, Abel Garr, Dan Jones, to find the company if possible, and report back their situation, whereabouts, etc.

Monday, October 27, 1856, Devil's Gate, The First Rescue Party, Daniel W. Jones Account. Having seen the sufferings of Brother Willie's company, we more fully realized the danger the others were in. The Elders who had just returned from England having many dear friends with these companies, suffered great anxiety, some of them feeling more or less the responsibility resting upon them for allowing these people to start so late in the season across the plains. At first we were at a loss what to do for we did not expect to have to go further than Devil's Gate. We decided to make camp and send on an express to find where the people were and not to return until they were found.

Joseph A. Young, Abe Garr and I were selected. (Some histories give other names, but I was there myself and am not mistaken.) With picked saddle horses and a pack mule we started out. The first night we camped, our horses followed a band of buffaloes several miles.

Tuesday, October 28, 1856, Red Buttes (about ten miles upstream from the Last Crossing of the Platte), The Express from the First Rescue Party, Daniel W. Jones Account. It was near noon the next day when we returned with [our horses]. We determined to get even with them so rode at full gallop wherever the road would permit. After riding about twelve miles we saw a white man's shoe track in the road. Bro. Young called out, "Here they are." We put our animals to their utmost speed and soon came in sight of the camp at Red Bluff [Red Buttes]. This was Brother Edward Martin's handcart company and Ben Hodgett's wagon company. There was still another wagon company [the Hunt Company] down near the Platte crossing.

Friday, October 31, 1856, Greasewood [Horse] Creek to Devil's Gate, The First Rescue Party, Daniel W. Jones Account. Next morning, Brother Young having come up, we three started for our camp near Devil's Gate. All were rejoiced to get the news that we had found the emigrants. The following morning most of the company moved down, meeting the handcart company at Greasewood [Horse] Creek. Such assistance as we could give was rendered to all until they finally arrived at Devil's Gate fort about the 1st of November. There were some twelve hundred in all, about one-half with handcarts and the other half with teams [Hodgett and Hunt Companies].

Martin Handcart Company, 1856

From the first of November, the Rescue Party was joined with the Martin Handcart Company and the Hunt and Hodgett Wagon Companies. Together, they made their way into Martin's Cove, where they tried to find shelter from the wind and cold. From that point forward, the story will be told as the story of the Martin Company, with additional reference to journals from the Rescue Party.

Saturday, November 1, 1856, Independence Rock, Martin Company, John Jaques Journal. On the evening of November 1st, the handcart company camped at the Sweetwater bridge, on this side of the river, about five miles on the other side [east] of Devil's Gate, arriving there about dark. There was a foot or eighteen inches of snow on the ground. As there were but one or two spades in camp, the emigrants had to shovel it away with their frying pans, or tin plates, or anything they could use for that purpose, before they could pitch their tents, and then the ground was frozen so hard that it was almost impossible to drive the tent pegs into it. Some of the men were so weak that it took them an hour or two to clear the places for their tents and set them up. They would shovel and scrape away the hard snow a few minutes and then rest, then shovel and rest again, and so on.

Saturday, November 1, 1856, near Independence Rock, Martin and Hodgett Companies, Jesse Haven Journal. Not very cold. Looks some like snow. It commenced snowing a little past noon. Soon camped for the night.

November 1856, Devil's Gate to South Pass, Martin Company, Alice Strong Walsh Account.[34] We arrived at Devil's Gate about the 1st of November on account of the nightly fatalities of the male members of our company for 2 or 3 weeks previously, there were many widows in our camp and the women and children had to pitch and put up the tents, shoveling the snow away with tin plates, etc. making our beds on the ground and getting up in the morning with melted snow and lie on our clothing. This hard service continued with all that were able to endure it till we nearly reached the south pass and one night I dropped to the ground in a dead faint with my baby in my arms. I had some pepper pods with me in recovering from my stupor I took some of them to warm and to recover my strength. During these times we had only a little thin flour gruel 2 or 3 times a day and this was meager nourishment for a mother with a nursing baby.

My husband died and was buried at or near Devil's Gate and the ground was frozen so hard that the men had a difficult task in digging the grave deep enough in which to inter him and nine others that morning, and it is more than probable that several were only covered over with snow. Here I was left a widow with 2 young children. The boy became so weak that he could not stand alone and I had to sit and hold both of them in the relief wagons from this on. At times the most of us had to walk after being met by the teams from Salt

---

[34] Sketch of Mrs. Alice Walsh Strong's Handcart Experience, written by Alice Walsh Strong and corrected by Josiah Rogerson.

Lake and late in the day, and towards the evening my shoes would nearly freeze to my feet and at one time in taking off, some of the skin and flesh came off with them. Some of the bones of my feet were left bare and my hands were severely frozen.

When the relief help reached us and nearly all of us had been assigned to some wagon, I was sitting in the snow with my children on my lap, and it seemed there was no chance for me to ride, but before the last teams had left the camp I was assigned to ride in the commissary wagon and did so until I arrived in Salt Lake City.

Sunday, November 2, 1856, Independence Rock to Devil's Gate, Hodgett Wagon Company, with Martin Company, Jesse Haven Journal. Sunday. Started this morning. Came to Independence Rock and found the handcart company there. Came on to Devil's Gate. It is an old trading post, some log cabins there. Took possession of them. About a mile from this post, the waters of the Sweetwater run between two perpendicular rocks, from 3 to 4 hundred feet high. This place is called Devil's Gate.

November, 1856, near Devil's Gate, Hunt Wagon Company, with the Martin and Hodgett Companies, Mary Goble Pay.[35] When we arrived at Devil's Gate it was bitter cold. We left many of our things there.... My brother James... was as well as he ever was when we went to bed that night. In the morning he was dead....

My feet were frozen; also my brother's and my sister's. It was nothing but snow. We could not drive the pegs in our tents.... We did not know what would become of us. Then

---

[35] As quoted by President Gordon B. Hinckley, Ensign, July 1984, p.6.

one night a man came to our camp and told us... Brigham Young had sent men and teams to help us.... We sang songs; some danced, and some cried.

Sunday, November 2, 1856, Devil's Gate, Martin Company, Patience Loader Account. One day I well remember we had a very hard day's travel. We arrived at Devil's Gate that night to camp in the snow which was deep and freezing. When we got to camp we found several big fires there and several log huts and several brethren from the valley were camping there. Brother Joel Parrish was cooking supper for the rest of the brethren. We were all so hungry and cold, many ran to get to the fire to warm but the brethren asked for all to be as patient as possible and we should have some wood to make us fires. Brother George Grant was there. He told us all to stand back for he was going to knock down one of those log huts to make fires for us. He said, "You are not going to freeze tonight." He raised his ax and with one blow knocked in the whole front of the building, took each log and split it in four pieces and gave each family one piece. Oh! such crowding for wood. Some would have taken more than one piece, but Brother Grant told them to hold on and not to be so greedy. There were some that had not got any yet. Brother Grant said, "There is one sister standing back waiting very patiently and she must have some," I said, "Yes, Brother Grant, my name is Patience and I have waited with patience." He laughed and said, "Give that sister some wood and let her go and make a fire." I was very thankful to get wood. I had stood so long that my clothing was stiff and my old stockings and shoes seemed frozen on my feet and legs. My poor mother was sitting down waiting until we got back with wood to make a fire. As soon as we could get the log cut in pieces we soon got our fire going and took off our wet stockings and dried them ready for morning. We had to wait some time before we got our flour for supper. During the time we were

91

waiting a good brother came to our camp fire and asked if we were all one family. We said we were six in number. Mother told him we were her daughters and the boy, her son. He asked if mother had no husband and she told him her husband had died two months ago and was buried on the plains. He had been standing with his hands behind him, then he handed us a piece of beef to cook for our supper. He left and came back with a beef bone. He said, "Here is a bone to make some soup and don't quarrel over it." We felt surprised that he should think we would ever quarrel over our food. Mother said, "Oh, brother, we never quarrel over having short rations, but we feel very thankful to you for giving us this meat for we had not got any meat, neither did we expect any."

Sunday, November 2, 1856, Devil's Gate, Martin Company, extracts from a letter written by George D. Grant, recorded in the Journal History. We had no snow to contend with, until we got to the Sweetwater. On the 19th and 20th of October we encountered a very severe snow storm. We met Brother Willie's company on the 21st. The snow was six to ten inches deep where we met them. They were truly in a bad situation, but we rendered them all the assistance in our power. Brother William H. Kimball returned with them, also several other brethren.

Previous to this time we had sent on an express to ascertain, if possible, the situation and whereabouts of the companies and report to me. Not thinking it safe for them to go farther than Independence Rock, I advised them to wait there. When we overtook them they had heard nothing from the rear companies, and we had traveled through snow from eight to twelve inches deep all the way from Willow Creek to this place.

Not having much feed for our horses, they were running down very fast, and, not hearing anything from the companies, I did not know but what they had taken up quarters for the winter, consequently we sent on another express to the Platte bridge. When the express returned, to my surprise I learned that the companies were all on the Platte river, near the upper crossing, [Red Buttes] and had been encamped there nine days, waiting for the snow to go away, or, as they said, to recruit their cattle. As quick as we learned this, we moved on to meet them. We met Brother Martin's company at Greasewood [Horse] Creek, on the last day of October. Brother Hodgett's company was a few miles behind [at Bad Slough]. We dealt out to Brother Martin's company the clothing, etc., that we had for them, and the next morning after stowing our wagons full of the sick, the children, and the infirm, with a good amount of luggage started homeward about noon. The snow began to fall very fast and continued until late at night. It is now about eight inches deep here and the weather is very cold. You can imagine between 500 and 600 men, women, and children worn down by drawing handcarts through snow and mud, fainting by the wayside; falling chilled by the cold; children crying, their limbs stiffened by cold, their feet bleeding and some of them bare to the snow and frost. The sight is almost too much for the stoutest of us. Our company is too small to help much. It is only a drop to a bucket as it were, in comparison with what is needed. I think that not over one-third of Martin's company is able to walk. This you may think is extravagant, but it is nevertheless true. Some of them have good courage, and are in good spirits, but a great many of them are like children, and do not help themselves much more, nor realize what is before them. Brother Chas. Decker has now traveled this road the forty-ninth time, and he says he has never before seen so much snow on the Sweetwater at any season of the year. Brother Hunt's company are two or three days back of us, yet Brother Wheelock [with Br. Broomhead] will be with them to counsel them, also some of the other brethren who came.

Sunday, November 2, 1856, Devil's Gate, Rescue Party, Journal History.   Soon Bro. Grant arrived and prepared the camp for moving. He said to Joseph A., "What would your father [Brigham Young] do now if he were here?" Joseph answered: "If my father was here he would take all the books and heavy material and cache them in order to save the lives of the people." So they agreed to do it. They cached all their articles at Devil's Gate and took up the feeble and started towards home.

Monday, November 3, 1856, Devil's Gate, Hodgett Company, Jesse Haven Journal. Weather cold, with 6 to 8 inches of snow on the ground.   The handcart company are camped here also.

November 1856, near Martin's Cove, Martin Company, Emily Cowley Fowler Recollection.[36]   Stories that thrill are told of the kindness and brotherly love that existed among these ill-fated pioneers. One of them mentioned in the different diaries gives an account of two men, the father and grandfather of Dr. George Middleton, who were in charge of the provision wagon of the Martin Company, picking up the children who were walking. They would tenderly take some of the babes from their mothers' arms and place them in the wagons. If one became discouraged because of physical pain, an hour's ride with the Middletons ofttimes brought courage back. Another interesting bit of history gives us the story of a beautiful courtship between one of the rescue party, William M. Cowley, and a lovely English girl, who was a member of Martin's Company. This young girl, Emily Wall, and her

---

[36] This entry is from the Family Recollection of Emily Cowley Fowler, a daughter of William Cowley of the Rescue Party and Emily Wall of the Martin Company.

brother Joseph started out for Utah well prepared to make the journey on foot, as their mother had purchased fifteen pairs of sturdy shoes for each of them. Emily was only fifteen years of age and her brother three years her senior, but they had been promised that they both would reach Salt Lake City. When the point was reached that their company could not carry so much, these two discarded part of their clothing, giving it to those who were not as fortunate as they. Part way across the plains the brother took ill and the company thought it best that he be left behind, telling the sister he could come on when he was better. However, Emily had been promised their safe arrival in the valley and she promised to pull her brother on her cart if he would only be permitted to come. Consent was given and with the aid of a small girl she pulled Joseph for three days. When she reached Devil's Gate where the company of rescuers met the party, one of the boys, William M. Cowley, who was a very young printer, came to her aid. In conversation with her he asked if some day she would marry him. Emily said she didn't know and told him he would have to write to England and get permission from her mother. Time went on and the youth was not seen again for three years, as he had been called to San Bernardino to set up a printing press. Upon his return he found the young lady at the home of President Young and asked her if she remembered his proposal. She had, but wanted to know if he had written to her mother. After being informed that a letter had been written to her mother and that an answer had come saying it was all right for them to be married provided he was a good man, Emily consented and the young couple were married. Twelve children were born to them and she remained his only sweetheart.

November 1856, near Martin's Cove, Martin Company, Margaret Pucell.[37] Samuel and Margaret Pucell and their two daughters were in the Martin Company. On the way Margaret became ill, so had to ride in the handcart part of the way. Her husband grew so weary and weakened from the lack of food that this additional burden caused him to slip and fall one day as he crossed a river. Having to travel in the cold, wintry weather with wet clothing he, too, became ill and died from hunger and exposure. His wife died five days later, leaving ten-year-old Ellen and fourteen-year-old Maggie orphans.... Many died and many others suffered from frozen limbs, among them the Pucell girls, both having badly frozen feet and legs.... When shoes and stockings were removed from the girls' feet the skin came off. Although Maggie's legs were frozen, she would not allow them to do more than scrape the flesh off the bones, but Ellen's were so bad they had to be amputated just below the knees. The girls stayed in Salt Lake waiting for their wounds to heal. Later they lived in Parowan for awhile, then on the Cedar, where both married and reared families, although Ellen Pucell (Unthanks) went on her knee-stubs all her life.

Monday, November 3, 1856, Devil's Gate, Rescue Party, R.T. Burton Account. Remained at same place. So cold that the company could not move. Sent an express to G.S.L. City, Joseph A. Young, and Abel Garr, to report our situation and get counsel and help.

Monday, November 3, 1856, Devil's Gate, Rescue Party, Journal History. The couriers again proved to be the tireless Joseph A. Young and Abel Garr. Before riding, Young put on three or four pairs of woollen socks, a pair of

---

[37] This entry is quoted from Hafen, Handcarts to Zion, p. 138.

moccasins, and a pair of buffalo hide over-shoes with the wool on, and then remarked, "There, if my feet freeze with those on, they must stay frozen till I get to Salt Lake."

Tuesday, November 4, 1856, Devil's Gate, Hodgett Company, Jesse Haven Journal. Thermometer 6 degrees below zero. Joseph A. Young and another brother started back on express this morning to the valley.

Tuesday, November 4, 1856, Devil's Gate to Martin's Cove, Martin Company, Journal History. Dan Jones wrote about the move: "The company was composed of average emigrants; old, middle aged and young; men, women and children. The men seemed to be failing and dying faster than the women and children. The handcart company was moved over to a cove in the mountains for shelter and fuel, a distance of two to three miles from Devil's Gate Fort to Martin's Cove. The wagons were banked near the fort. It became impossible to travel further without reconstruction or help. We did all we possibly could to help and cheer the people."

Tuesday, November 4, 1856, Devil's Gate to Martin's Cove, Martin Company, Patience Loader Account. The handcart company was in part reorganized, and most of the carts were left there [Devil's Gate], two of the best being retained for each hundred. These were loaded with cooking utensils, such as frying pans, bake kettles, saucepans, and camp kettles, so that the loads in these few carts were of a weighty nature. The remainder of the baggage of the company was put on the wagons. Under this arrangement the company started from Devil's Gate westward and when about three miles away crossed the Sweetwater to the north side and camped at a place known since as Martin's Ravine. It was not exactly a ravine, but a recess or opening in the mountains, which here run along near the river. The passage of the Sweetwater at this point was a severe operation to many of the company. It was the worst river crossing of the expedition and the last. The water was not less than two feet deep, perhaps a little more in the deepest parts, but it was intensely cold. The ice was three or four inches thick, and the bottom of the river muddy or sandy. I forget exactly how wide the stream was there, but I think thirty or forty yards. It seemed a good deal wider than that to those who pulled their handcarts through it. Before the crossing was completed, the shades of evening were closing around, and, as everybody knows, that is the coldest hour of the twenty-four, or at least it seemed to be so, in a frosty time, and it seemed so then for cold enough it was. The teams and wagons and handcarts and some of the men forded the river. Four members of the relief party waded the river, helping the handcarts through and carrying the women and children and some of the weaker men over. They were D. P. Kimball[38],

---

[38] David P. Kimball was the fourth son of Heber C. and Vilate Kimball born on August 23, 1839. He was named, David Patton, after David W. Patton, president of the Council of Twelve Apostles. His mother penned the following lines for the benefit of her husband who was on his second mission to England:

> Our darling little David P.
> Is just as sweet as he can be;
> He surely is the finest lad
> That you and I have ever had.
>
> His eyes are black, his skin is fair,
> His features good, and brown his hair;
> He's just as fat as butter, too,
> We therefore think that he will do.

One of the great acts of heroism in Church History was performed by David P. Kimball and his twenty-seven associates who on the morning of October 7, 1856, left Salt Lake City to the relief of

George W. Grant, Stephen W. Taylor, and C. A. Huntington.

In the rear part of the company, two men were pulling one of the handcarts, assisted by two or three women, for the women pulled as well as the men all the way so long as the handcarts lasted. When the handcart arrived at the bank of the river, one of these men who was much worked down, asked in a plaintive tone, "Have we got to go through there?" On being answered yes, he was so much affected that he was completely overcome. That was the last strain. His fortitude and manhood gave way. He exclaimed, "Oh, dear! I can't go through that," and burst into tears. His wife, who was by his side, had the stouter heart of the two at that juncture, and she said soothingly, "Don't cry, Jimmy. I'll pull the cart for you." A noble and generous offer which was not carried out. Jimmy besought one of the "boys" from "the valley," who was in the water, to carry him over. The "boy" urged that the women and children had the first claim, but finally consented to carry him across. Jimmy got on the back of the "boy" to ride over, and the "boy" started with him. This little episode, however, ended badly for Jimmy, for, before he was carried entirely across the "boy" slipped and fell with Jimmy into the water, very wet water it was too and very cold, freezingly cold, enough to congeal anything. When the river was forded, he found that Jimmy and the women assigned to help pull the cart were all gone on to the camp at the base of the mountains,

---

hundreds of belated handcart emigrants caught in the early snows of this severe winter. David Kimball along with others, carried nearly every member of the Martin Company across the Sweetwater into Martin's Cove. When President Brigham Young heard of this heroic act, he wept like a child, and later declared, "that act alone will insure David P. Kimball, George W. Grant and C. Allen Huntington an everlasting salvation in the Celestial Kingdom of God, worlds without end." (Solomon F. Kimball, Life of David P. Kimball, pp. 1-9)

from half a mile to a mile distant. The way to camp was over rising ground, covered with sage brush, and with about a foot of snow on the surface. All alone he pulled his heavy laden cart over the snow and clumps of brush, for road there was none, till he reached the camp. Going through the river and taking his cart single handed to camp after he had affected the crossing of the river, on that piercing cold evening, was the hardest piece of tugging he had encountered on the entire journey, and it was the last on the journey, which was much better. When he arrived in camp, he had to climb the mountain to cut some cedar for firewood. The "boys" of the relief party had cut some wood for the camp, but that had all been appropriated before he arrived in camp. So he went on the mountain, and the mountains there are little else than rocks, and he took his little hatchet, for axes were few in the camp. Green cedar was of little use. Nothing but dry cedar was really serviceable for fuel, and the dry cedar was almost as hard as iron, while his hatchet had not been ground since he left the Missouri, if it had since he left Iowa City. So I will leave you to imagine how long he was that night before he succeeded in getting fuel for those depending on him.

One brother took the cart and another helped us girls over the water and said we should not wade the cold water any more and tried to encourage us by saying soon we would all be able to ride in wagons. We traveled on for some few miles, then we came to the Sweetwater River and there we had to cross. We thought we should have to wade as the cattle had been crossing with the wagons with the tents and what little flour we had and had broken the ice. But there were brave men there in the water, packing the women and children over on their backs. Those brethren were in the water all day. We wanted to thank them but they would not listen to my dear mother who felt in her heart to bless them for their kindness. She said, "God bless you for taking me over this water," and they said in such an awful rough way, "Oh, d--n that. We

100

don't want any of that. You are welcome, We have come to help you." Mother turned to me, saying, "What do you think of that man, Patience? He is a rough fellow." I told her, "That is Brother Kimball, I am told. They are all good men, but I dare say they are rather rough in their manners." But we found that they all had good, kind hearts. This poor Brother [David P.] Kimball stayed so long in the water that he had to be taken out and packed to camp and he was a long time before he recovered as he was chilled through and in after life he was always afflicted with rheumatism.

After we were over the Sweetwater we had to travel some distance to a good camping place. We had a very nice camping place. (In the early part of the journey and until the relief party was met, the camps were made in open situations, as a rule, with a special view to avoid, as much as possible, being surprised or ambushed by Indians. Afterward, sheltered spots were chosen, with a view to make the company as comfortable as possible in camp.) Here we remained for 9 days as we had to wait until more provisions came to us. Supplies had to be left at Devil's Gate for the brethren that had to stay all winter. The cattle had nearly all given out, both in the wagon companies and our company and a great deal of freight had to be left there until spring. We were on four ounces of flour a day nearly all the time we were in camp on the Sweetwater, but the morning we had orders to leave there, we were told to leave our handcarts. We were all very glad to leave the cart, but we had to walk for several days before we could all ride in the wagons.... We got dear mother in the wagon to ride and we girls were good and willing to walk until such time as it would be convenient for us to ride. During our 9 days stay on the Sweetwater many of the stout young men went out and got rawhide and anything they could eat. On one occasion I got a bone given me with scarcely any meat on it. I was cooking it to make a little soup for breakfast and the brethren from the Valley came and asked me to go to their camp and sing songs for them. so I left mother to see to the cooking of the bone and my sisters went with me. The brethren had cut down logs and formed seats for us all around the camp fire, but they said they had nothing to give us to eat as they themselves were short of food. Well, we sang and enjoyed ourselves for 2 or 3 hours and then we went to our tent. When we arrived there our fire was out and mother had gone to bed and my ten year old brother was also in bed. Mother said, "I fetched the pot with the soup," We said, "Alright mother. We stayed longer than we ought to, but the brethren did not want us to leave, but we told them we would go and sing for them another night." We were so hungry but we had nothing to eat and it makes you hungry to sing. [Mother said,] "You had better not go to sing for the brethren again. I must tell you, I got so hungry that I took the bone out of your soup and picked the little meat off it and put the bone back into the pot. It seemed that I could not go to sleep without telling you, for I knew you would not find anything on the bone in the morning." We told her that was all right. We felt glad that our dear mother found a little bit to eat and we all went to sleep and slept comfortable and warm until morning, notwithstanding it was a terrible cold, freezing night.

Tuesday, November 4, 1856, Devil's Gate to Martin's Cove, Hunt Company (with the Martin Company), Journal History. The weather being a little milder, the company resumed the journey at 12 o'clock noon, crossing the Sweetwater and camped at 4 p.m., having traveled 6 miles. Twenty-four wagons were the number taken by the company from Devil's Gate.

November, 1856, near Devil's Gate, Hunt Company (with the Martin and Hodgett Companies), Elizabeth White.[39] It was getting very cold.... We were almost out of provisions.... Our two yoke of oxen and one cow had died and the rest of the company were in about the same condition. We had nothing to burn only the wet sage brush from under the snow and melt the snow off the sage for our water to make our tea. We made our bread with soda and sage water what little we had. The snow was then from three to ten inches deep. The ground was frozen so hard they could not drive the tent pins so they had to raise the tent poles and stretch out the flaps and bank them down with snow. Our dear mother said she had never seen her family want for bread, but said the Lord would provide. About midnight that night all had retired and we were awakened with a noise... to our great surprise the noise was caused by the teamsters of a relief train and some of the camp shouted for joy.... I remember we had to cut everything with the hatchet but oh how thankful we all were that the Lord had answered our prayers and saved us all from starvation.... George Clawson and Gurnsey Brown were the teamsters.

November 1856, near Martin's Cove, Martin Company, Elizabeth Sermon Recollections.[40] My husband's health began to fail and his heart almost broken to see me falling in shafts. Myself and children hungry, almost naked, footsore and himself nearly done for. Many trials came after this. My oldest boy had the mountain fever, we had to haul

---

[39] Autobiography of Elizabeth White Stewart, found in Barnard White Family Book; prepared and edited by Ruth Johnson and Glen F. Harding, BYU Press.

[40] This account is taken from Elizabeth Sermon's Emigration and Journey Across the Plains, a history written by herself to her son Henry.

him in the cart, there was not room in the wagon. One day we started him out before the carts in the morning to walk with the aged and sick, but we had not gone far on our journey before we found him lying by the roadside, unable to go any farther. I picked him up and put him on my back and drew my cart as well, but could not manage far, so put him in the cart, which made three children and my luggage. My husband failing more each day, the Captain put a young man to help me for a short time. My other son Henry walked at 7 years old, 1300 miles with the exception of a few miles....

I will here state there was no time crossing the rivers to stop and take off clothing, but had to wade through and draw our carts at the same time with our clothes dripping wet, had to dry in the sun and dust as merrily on our way we go until we reach the valley, oh, like a herd of stock or something worse....

Many cruel and painful things happening, the dying and dear ones all around us, poor souls, would sit down by the roadside and would never move again until carried into camp on handcarts by someone. It is a wonder any of us lived through it. My husband's health still failing, a young woman by the name of Caroline Marchant assisted me with the cart.... Not far from here [Devil's Gate] the Captain called us together to tell us we must lay our bodies down. Were we willing to do so for the Gospel's sake? Many poor half-starved men shouted with what remaining strength they had, "Aye." But mothers could not say that and were quiet. We went back to our tents, food would have suited us then. My faith was in my Heavenly Father. I never lost that faith in Him. It is as sweet today to trust and my prayer is, may I always trust Him. He is a friend that has never failed.

My husband's sufferings have always pained me and I can never forget them. Poor Rob's [age 5] feet began to freeze. I cannot remember the place; it was after wading a very deep river [Platte?] the freezing commenced. We had no wood but sagebrush. I went out and cut the sage to keep the fire all night. Covered them up with their feet to the fire and cut some more and kept the fire as well as I could. My clothes froze stiff. Well, we got through that night. Your father would not walk now. He would get into wagon after wagon, only to be turned out. The cattle were giving out and everyone had their friends, but the friend death, would soon end his sufferings. John [age 9] and Rob had to ride, Henry [age 7] walked, your father would take my arm and walk a little distance, fall on his knees with weakness. We moved from Devil's Gate. I believe it was brother David Kimball who carried us over a river [Sweetwater] and a great many more besides us. My poor husband blessed him for so doing.

After our food had given out as I said before, we went to our tents to die. I always thought I could get through to Salt Lake City and I tried to encourage my husband, but he was starving. He had always lived good at home. There was a shout in the camp. Brother Joseph A. Young had come on packed mules with Brother Little. Brought flour, meat and onions. I got 1 pound of flour and some meat and 2 onions. I chopped the fat off the meat real fine and made some dumplings. We made a good meal and blessed Brother Little and Joseph from the bottom of our hearts.... We had 70 miles to get to the wagons that had been sent from Salt Lake City with food and clothing and some clothing had come for us. Your father after having some food and clothes, seemed to revive. He called you to him and told you to be good children and to do all you could for me, and then he said to me, "God bless you, Eli," that being the name he called me. "You have saved my life this time."

I said, "We must hold out now and get to the wagons," but we had to go back to the 1/4 lb. of flour and he sank under it. I think he would not have died if he had got food, but he was spared the trial ahead. We went to bed about 3:00. He put his arm around me and said, "I am done," and breathed his last. I called Brother John Oley. We sewed him up in a quilt with his clothes on, except his boots, which I put on my feet and wore them into Salt Lake City. A coat I put on John to keep him warm, which afterward went to Ft. Bridger. Some friend tried to get it for me but we did not succeed. Father was buried in the morning with 2 more in the grave. I stood like a statue, bewildered, not a tear: the cold chills, even now as I write, creep over my body, for I feel I can still see the wolves waiting for their bodies as they would come down to camp before we left.

Well, I went again to the cart as all that could had to walk to get to the wagons. Poor Rob had to ride from this time and sometimes John, Henry and Marian [age 3] were with me. When I got into camp I would clear the snow away with a tin plate, gather my wood, get my bed clothes from the wagon.... I was too weak to haul much....get my allowance of flour and carry the children to the fire, make their beds on the ground, the tent was frozen and ground so hard we could not set it up. I think it was two weeks we were without tents. We went to bed without supper in order to get a little better breakfast. I found it some help to toast the rawhide on the coals and chew it; it helped to keep the hunger away, for I was feeling it rather keenly now. I had to take a portion of poor Robert's feet off which pierced my very soul. I had to sever the leaders with a pair of scissors. Little did I think when I bought them in old England that they would be used for such a purpose. Every day some portion was decaying until the poor boy's feet were all gone. Then John's began to freeze; then afterwards my own. We kept meeting teams from Salt Lake City now, which rendered all the assistance they could. I remember asking one of the drivers if he could give me a cob of corn to eat. He looked so pitiful and said, "Oh, sister, I hate to refuse you but my horses haven't enough to eat now, and I do not know how we will get back to Salt Lake." I said, "I ought not to have asked you, but myself and children

106

are so hungry." He said, "Keep up your faith sister."

A loaf of bread would have given me great faith and satisfied a hungry stomach as well, but the bread was not many miles off. We got it and it was the sweetest bread we ever ate. One instance occurred. Poor Brother Blair, a very tall thin man; he was starving and was eating a piece of griddle cake; another poor brother, not as hungry asked for a piece of it. He said, "I cannot do it, I want it myself." Poor fellow, he died in the night and so one after another passed away. Fathers, mothers, sisters, brothers and friends, many, many honest souls laid in mother earth. The brothers kept meeting us and some times we had a good cheery fire built for us when we got into camp. I was terribly put to for clothes to wrap my poor boy's legs in, his feet all gone. I got all I could from the camp, then I used my underclothing until I had but 2 skirts left upon my body, and as such I finished my journey for my wardrobe would not be replenished where I was.

At last the old handcart was laid by without a regret; we got to the wagons, were taken in and some days we rode all day and got a little more food. A severe storm came up. I think it was on the Sweetwater, but I was so troubled I forget all about the names of places. My eldest boy John's feet decaying, my boys both of them losing their limbs, their father dead, my own feet very painful, I thought, "Why can't I die?" My first thought of death. Brother Patton took us in his wagon, blessed me for my integrity and blessed us with tea and bread and so with what food was so kindly sent out to us from the people in Salt Lake, our lives were spared.

Wednesday, November 5, 1856, Martin's Cove, Martin Company, John Jaques Journal. The handcart company rested in Martin's Ravine. Though under the shelter of the northern mountains, it was a cold place. One night the gusty wind blew over a number of tents, and it was with difficulty some of the emigrants could keep from freezing to

107

death. One afternoon Captain Martin and 2 or 3 other men started to go from the camp to Devil's Gate, but a snow storm came on and they mistook their bearings and lost their way. After wandering about for several hours, they came near perishing. In their exigency they endeavored to make a fire to warm themselves. They gathered some cedar twigs and struck match after match to light them, but in vain. At length with their last match and the aid of portions of their body linen they succeeded in starting a fire. This was seen from the handcart camp, from which, after all their anxious and weary wanderings, they were only about half a mile distant. Help soon came to the benighted wanderers and the "boys" carried Captain Martin, who was nearly exhausted, back to camp.

Thursday, November 6, 1856, Devil's Gate, Hodgett Company, Jesse Haven Journal. Weather some warmer near Devil's Gate. Very cold. Thermometer stood at 6 degrees below zero.

Sunday, November 9, 1856, Martin's Cove, The First Rescue Party and the Martin Company, R.T. Burton Account. Fine, warm morning. Handcart company and Captain Hodgett's company at 11 o'clock a.m. Captain Hunt's company not yet done caching goods. This evening had a meeting of the officers of the companies to appoint brethren to remain with the goods, left here by Captains Hodgett's and Hunt's companies. Dan Jones left in charge or president, F.M. Alexander and Benjamin Hampton counselors, with 17 other brethren from the two companies. The brethren were instructed in their duties. During our stay here, we had meetings every evening to counsel together and ask the Lord to turn away the cold and storm, so that people might live.

Sunday, November 9, 1856, Martin's Cove, The First Rescue Party and the Martin Company, Daniel W. Jones Account. Steve Taylor, Al Huntington and I were together when the question, "Why doesn't Captain Grant leave all the goods here with some one to watch, and move on?" was asked. We agreed to make this proposal to him. It was near the time appointed for the meeting. As soon as we were together, Capt. Grant asked if anyone had thought of a plan. We presented ours. Capt. Grant replied, "I have thought of this, but there are no provisions to leave and it would be asking too much of anyone to stay here and starve for the sake of these goods; besides, where is there a man who would stay if called upon." I answered, "Any of us would." I had no idea I would be selected as it was acknowledged I was the best cook in camp and Captain Grant had often spoken as though he could not spare me.

That a proper understanding may be had, I will say that these goods were the luggage of a season's emigration that these two wagon trains had contracted to freight, and it was being taken through as well as the luggage of the people present. Leaving these goods meant to abandon all that many poor families had upon earth. So it was different from common merchandise.

There was a move made at once to adopt this suggestion. Accordingly, next morning store rooms in the fort were cleared and some two hundred wagons run in and unloaded. No one was allowed to keep out anything but a change of clothing, some bedding and light cooking utensils. Hauling provisions was not a weighty question.

This unloading occupied three days. The handcart people were notified to abandon most of their carts. Teams were hitched up and the sick and feeble loaded in with such light weight as was allowed. All became common property.

When everything was ready Brother Burton said to me, "Now Brother Jones we want you to pick two men from the

109

valley to stay with you. We have notified Captains Hunt and Hodgett to detail seventeen men from their companies to stay with you. We will move on in the morning. Get your company together and such provisions as you can find in the hands of those who may have anything to spare. You know ours is about out. Will you do it?" I said, "Yes." "Well, take your choice from our company. You are acquainted with the boys and whoever you want will stay." I had a great mind to tell him I wanted Captains Grant and Burton.

There was not money enough on earth to have hired me to stay. I had left home for only a few days and was not prepared to remain so long away; but I remembered my assertion that any of us would stay if called upon. I could not back out, so I selected Thomas Alexander and Ben Hampton. I am satisfied that two more faithful men to stand under all hardships could not have been found.

On taking stock of provisions, we found about twenty day's rations. No salt or bread excepting a few crackers. There was at least five months of winter before us and nothing much to eat but a few perishing cattle and what game we might chance to kill. The game was not very certain, as the severe storms had driven everything away. The first move was to fix up the fort. Accordingly Brother Alexander, being a practical man, was appointed to manage the business; Brother Hampton was to see about the cattle.

Sunday, November 9, 1856, Martin's Cove, The First Rescue Party and the Martin Company, John Jaques Journal. At Devil's Gate an earnest council was held to determine whether to endeavor to winter the emigrants at that point, or to push them on to Salt Lake as fast as possible. It was decided to continue the march to Salt Lake. When the wagon companies had come up to Devil's Gate it was decided to store most of the freight at that point for the winter which was done, and twenty men were left, under the direction of

Daniel W. Jones, to take care of the goods. Those twenty men had a hard time of it before they were relieved the following summer and the goods brought along to Salt Lake, for there was not sufficient supplies that could be spared to provision the men with the amount and variety they ought to have had. The freight was left behind because the teams were unable to haul it further. The great object now was to save as many of the people as possible, to which everything else must give way, and the lives of the people depended in a great degree on the lives of the teams and on their strength, so it was essential to spare the animals all unnecessary labor.

Devil's Gate, November 9, 1856: Minutes of a meeting of the Elders called at the request of Captain Grant to appoint men to remain in charge of goods left for storage at this place by Captain Hodgett's and Captain Hunt's wagon companies. Meeting opened by singing and prayer by Elder Daniel W. Jones after which the following persons were appointed to remain--viz., Daniel W. Jones, Thomas M. Alexander, Benjamin Hampton, John Cooper, George Walts, Elisha Manning, George Allen, George Austin, William Hansley, John W. Latey, William Latey, John Shorten, John Weltarker, Edwin Summers, John Hardcastle, Henry Iverkinan, Rosser Jenkins and Elijah L. Chappel.

On the motion of Elder Cyrus H. Wheelock, Elder Daniel W. Jones was appointed President of the company remaining and Thomas M. Alexander and Benjamin Hampton his councilors and John H. Latey the clerk, after which the following instructions were given.

Captain Grant addressed the meeting saying that we were met together to arrange matters relating to the safe keeping of the luggage left here. It was a great trust reposed in those men appointed to remain but men with large souls, men of integrity, men of God who would not do a wrong thing, would not steal one from another if any. If any such were among them, he wanted them to be passed through the

Devil's Gate and he did not want any grumblers or fault finders, and he did not want one of the company to be the butt of the others because he may not be so smart. He wanted them to agree together and be obedient to the brethren who have come from the valleys and were called to preside over them for they were good men, had been cradled in Mormonism and had the spirit of Zion burning within them. He believed the men remaining were good men and would not do anything wrong. Wished them to improve their time that they might come up to Zion in the spring with the spirit of God increased in them, wished them to attend to their prayers not only night and morning but on the mountain tops to remember to call on the Lord mightily that his mind might be revealed to them and that they might be blessed. They could kill buffalo and antelope. He wanted the twenty left here to sleep with one eye open and one leg out of bed for there were devils, mountaineers and Indians round about here and a guard would be necessary if only one man at a time and if Indians were prowling two men would be necessary and the guards he wanted to be vigilant and not to sleep at their posts for the lives of their brethren were in their hands, and if they were killed the blood would be on their garments. Wanted them to have water in their vessels at all times, wanted these old shanties to be repaired and made comfortable and good. The guns also to be kept in good order and loaded and not lying all in a pile but every man knowing where to put his hand on his own gun and if Indians were prowling about, did not want them to fool with them. Word would be sent from the Valley before the spring and the provisions here he wanted to have rationed out and take care of the flour in portion. Wished them to be obedient to the counsels of President Jones and he wanted President Jones to maintain the dignity of his calling and not joke too much or suffer himself to be joked with for he knew where a man in office joked with those under him so sure was he to lose his influence. Did not wish any families to remain here for if

112

women and children remained there would be the devil to pay and there was not much prospect of anything for them to eat but meat, wanted those remaining to see that each other did not get lost and frozen to death. Wanted care taken of the wagons and cattle and not use the latter in hauling firewood but use the handcarts--expected the heifers left would improve in condition.

Monday, November 10, 1856, Martin's Cove, Martin and Hunt Companies and the Rescue Party, Journal History. Mary Hutchinson, aged 70 years, died at 4 o'clock p.m. James Reese, aged 60 years, died at 9 o'clock p.m. after suffering a long time from diarrhea and ague.

November 1856, vicinity of Martin's Cove, Martin Company, Journal of Langley Allgood Bailey. On leaving this morning my brother John saw the wolves devouring the bodies he had helped to bury the day before. He tried to drive them away [but] he had to run for his life. That morning in starting I was placed in a wagon on top of frozen tents.... Made about 4 miles. When the company stopped that evening mother came around the wagons calling lamely. I could hear her calling but she could not hear me answer. When she found me, [and] lifted me out of the wagon, my legs and arms [were] stiff like a frozen shirt. An ox was about to die. He was killed [and] mother got some of the meat, boiled it and gave me some of the broth. It ran through me like going through a funnel.

CHAPTER 3
THE TRAIL
TO COTTONWOOD CREEK

A prominent landmark along this section of the trail is a nearby peak that is called **Split Rock** because it has a notch that is clearly visible from a great distance. It has the appearance of an old-fashioned gun sight, and has a fascinating Indian legend associated with it. Local legends have a purely geographical significance, since the Indian's active imagination is capable of supplying explanations for any unknown phenomenon. This enormous rock, in the Granite Mountains near the Sweetwater River, is cleft vertically from top to bottom, evidence enough to prove to the Shoshonis that it must have been the work of a super-human power. In one version of the legend, a trapper jumped into a depression in the ground to avoid being crushed by a tumbling rock. Crouching, he expected it to roll on him, but to his horror, it came to rest immediately above him. Nighthawk responded to his call for help and summoned Lightning, who with one swift stroke severed the rock and freed the trapper. The paleface showed his ingratitude by devouring the first object in sight--the unfortunate Nighthawk. In this interesting legend, the Shoshonis actually had a three-fold purpose. They explained the mystery of the cleft; showed distrust in the white man; and gave the reason for the unusual sound the Nighthawk makes as it darts about at dusk in search of bugs.[41]

As the trail continues west along the Sweetwater River, it passes **Cottonwood Creek**. Cottonwood Creek today is part of the Hat Ranch owned by Virginia McIntosh. The ranch was

---

[41] See Beebe, Ruth, "Reminiscing Along the Sweetwater".

114

originally a homestead of P.J. McIntosh, beginning in 1885. He built his ranch house only 300 feet from the old Oregon Trail. One of his children, William "Bill" McIntosh, was the first white child born of resident parents on the Sweetwater River. Bill passed away in May, 1995. He is survived by his widow, Virginia and their daughter. Their family has a great love for their country, their state, and the heritage of the Oregon/Mormon trail.

1847 Pioneer Company

Wednesday, June 23, 1847, Cottonwood Creek, Pioneer Company, William Clayton. Morning fine and warm. After breakfast I went to the top of the high bluff expecting to get a good view of the country west but was disappointed in consequence of the many ridges or bluffs but a little distance beyond us. At seven o'clock the camp moved forward and immediately after saw a graveyard on the left of the road with a board stuck up with these words written on it: "Matilda Crowley, B. July 16th, 1830, and D. July 7, 1846." On reflecting afterward that some of the numerous emigrants who had probably started with a view to spend the remainder of their days in the wild Oregon, had fallen by the way and their remains had to be left by their friends far from the place of destination, I felt a renewed anxiety that the Lord will kindly preserve the lives of all my family, that they may be permitted to gather to the future home of the Saints, enjoy the society of the people of God for many years to come, and when their days are numbered that their remains may be deposited at the feet of the servants of God, rather than be left far away in a wild country. And oh, Lord, grant this sincere desire of thy servant in the name of Thy Son Jesus. Amen. After traveling one and a half miles we crossed a very shoal stream of clear, cold water about five feet wide. There is but little grass here although a number of bitter cottonwood trees grow on the banks. There being no name on the map for this creek, it was named Bitter Cottonwood Creek [referred to today as Cottonwood Creek] to designate it in our future travel. It is probable that this stream is caused by the melting of the snow on the mountains and if so, could not be depended on for a camp ground late in the summer. After passing this creek, the river runs between some of the high rocky ridges, the road at the same time bending a little southwest to pass around them. After traveling five miles beyond the last mentioned creek, we again descended to the banks of the river where would be a pretty good camp ground although the grass is not so plentiful as in many other places on the banks of the river. We traveled till 11:05 on the river banks than halted for noon where the road and river separated a little farther and hence we would probably not find grass again for a number of miles. The land continues very sandy, making it hard on teams; our course about west, the day very warm with a light south breeze. We traveled eight and a half miles this morning.

Wednesday, June 23, 1847, Cottonwood Creek, Pioneer Company, George A. Smith. Wednesday, June 23. Some cloudy, but quite warm. Started at 7 a.m. and passed just at our left the headboard of a grave marked "Matilda Crowley, b. July 16th, 1830, d. July 7, 1846." In one mile and a half crossed a run five feet wide, called Cottonwood Creek, passed just on our right a short low isolated wall of calcareous sandstone [this formation is still visible, along with distinctive ruts in the trail nearby].... Opposite this point the left range...for some distance affords an extended view of the country, beyond which appears dry and treeless and quite level plain by its outline against the sky. The bottom is quite level to the base of the right ridge and densely covered with thrifty absinthine. Passed a low range of granite on our right, and just beyond it turned to the river again. Noon halt at the issuing of the river between two sloping granite walls [this

116

location is referred to as the Three Crossings of the Sweetwater]. Grass good. Road heavy from sand and gravel, although pretty good. Distance 8 1/2 miles.

Willie Handcart Company, 1856

Thursday, October 16, 1856, Between Devil's Gate and Three Crossings of the Sweetwater, Willie Company, William Woodward, Clerk. "Early this morning sister Ella, wife of Olof Wicklund was delivered of a son. George Curtis, from Norton, Gloucestershire, England, aged 64 years died; Lars Julius Larsen, who was born July 5th, 1856, in camp at Iowa City died. John Roberts from Bristol, Somersetshire, England, aged 42 years died. The camp rolled on, roads hilly & sandy, nooned after travelling about 5 miles; rolled on & camped on the banks of the Sweetwater. Many of our company are failing in health. Feed for the cattle scarce. Came about 11 miles."

Thursday, October 16, 1856, Between Devil's Gate and Three Crossings of the Sweetwater, Willie Company, Levi Savage Journal. "Sweetwater. This morning we had three deaths and one birth. We have traveled eleven miles today. Our oxen are much worn down and our loadings were used daily by the weak and sick."

Ephraim Hanks Rescue Mission, 1856

Ephraim Hanks was one of the premier frontiersman of his day. He joined the rescue effort after the First Rescue Party was already on their way east. It was at Cottonwood Creek that Ephraim Hanks first encountered the Martin Company. The story of his life and how he came to be part of the rescue effort is an important part of understanding why he

117

was so successful in providing both physical and spiritual relief to the suffering emigrants.

The following illustrates the way in which the great quality of obedience was part of the character of this legendary pioneer: "On many occasions Ephraim Hanks was rewarded for his obedience to the Prophet Brigham Young. One spring morning he was at work, building an adobe house in the city. The basement was almost completed and he was just beginning to lay the sun-dried brick when Brigham drove up in his carriage and said, 'Ephraim, how thick is that rock wall?' Ephraim answered that is was eight inches thick. Brigham said, 'Tear it all down, Ephraim, and build it twice as thick.' Then as if to avoid argument, he turned his carriage around and drove away. Ephraim had been hauling rock from Ensign Peak for many days, and had paid a mason a good price to lay it in lime mortar. He dreaded the extra work and expense of doing it all over again. The mason, too, showed his disapproval by swearing and remarking, 'Brigham Young may be a saint, but he's no kind of a prophet about building stone walls.' Nevertheless, Ephraim re-contracted with the stonemason to double the wall, and the next morning started hauling rock again. A month later they had laid on this sixteen-inch wall much adobe brick and mud. As they were putting up the rafters, a terrific storm started. Rain fell in sheets causing streamlets of water to run in all directions. In a few minutes the basement of the new house was flooded, but the sturdy, thick walls stood safe and strong, supporting the house. A few days later when the water had drained out and they finished laying the rafters, Ephraim drove in the nails to the tune of 'We Thank Thee, Oh God, For a Prophet.'

"Many times President Brigham Young called men to do things as a test of their faith. One evening at a dance, Brigham called Ephraim over to him and asked him to go home and shave. Like all the strong, virile men of that day, Ephraim wore a long beard. It was brown and wavy and almost reached his waist. Without a question, he walked home, and after a last look in the mirror and a gentle stroke of his favored possession, he went to work with scissors and razor. He left, however, a mustache but even with that, as he stated afterwards, he looked 'like a peeled onion.' Hurrying back to the hall, he was greeted with laughter by everyone but Brigham, who frowned and said, 'Did I ask you to shave?' Ephraim nodded. 'Well, then, go back and do it right,' Brigham demanded, with a gesture of his hand across his entire face. Without a word of remonstrance, Ephraim did as he was told. President Young discovered that here was a man who would give him strict obedience, regardless of the nature of the request. Here was a man who could be trusted with the most important missions and who would serve in an exacting manner."[42]

Ephraim Hanks showed remarkable resourcefulness as he faced challenges. "[On] one occasion Eph and Charley [Decker] were caught in a fearful snowstorm, which blockaded their way for twelve days. They were well supplied with provisions, and managed to get into a cave with their animals, where they safely remained on pieces of jerked meat rolled in flour.... On another occasion their provisions gave out, and as their ammunition had become wet, while crossing a river, they were unable to shoot game. There were plenty of fat buffalo nearby, however, and they were determined to have some fresh meat, even though to obtain it they must engage in hazardous adventure. Eph, possessing a good horse and being a born athlete, chased after a big fat buffalo, ran his horse close to its

---

[42] E. Hanks, "Scouting For The Mormons On The Great Frontier." Deseret News Press, pp. 78-81.

side, then with both hands grabbed its mane, jumped astride, and while the animal was running at full speed, Eph with all his might drove his long knife into the buffalo's heart. This thrilling episode over, they jerked the meat and continued on their journey as if nothing unusual had occurred. These two men each crossed the plains probably more times than any other white man. They performed the perilous journey upwards of sixty times."

Several times his life was saved, he declared, through the guidance of dreams.[43] Ephraim Hanks also possessed the gift of healing to a remarkable degree, and always carried a small bottle of consecrated oil. Often he administered to the sick Indians, with powerful results. To them, from Salt Lake City to the Missouri River, he was known as the man who could talk with the Great Spirit. One particular incident occurred during the winter of 1857, when Eph was carrying the mail from Salt Lake City to Independence, Missouri. "A large tribe of Sioux were encamped a short distance away, and Elder Hanks felt impressed to visit them. As soon as he reached their camp he made his way to the chief's tent, where he found no one present except an elderly female. Soon, however, the chief came, and the lodge was filled with representative members of the tribe. As Ephraim took his place among them, the chief wanted to know who he was, and where he had come from. Elder Hanks answered that he lived in the mountains and belonged to the people who had pulled handcarts across the plains, that his chief's name was Brigham Young, who sometimes talked with the Great Spirit. The chief then wanted to know if Hanks himself could talk with the Great Spirit, which question the scout answered in the affirmative. The chief then spoke a few words to the assembled warriors, after which

---

[43] Improvement Era, Vol. XI, Sept., 1908, p. 839.

a number of them left the lodge and in a few moments returned, carrying an Indian boy in the blanket. It seems that the boy, while out on a buffalo hunt, had been thrown from his horse. His back was so badly injured that he had not been able to move for months. The chief, pointing to the boy, asked Elder Hanks if he would talk to the Great Spirit in behalf of the injured lad, which Ephraim consented to do. After the clothing had been removed from the boy's body, Elder Hanks anointed the afflicted parts with consecrated oil, which he always carried with him, and then administered to him in the name of Jesus Christ, promising that he should be made whole from that very moment. The boy immediately arose from his bed of affliction and walked out of the lodge, to the astonishment of all who saw."[44]

Friday, October 24, 1856, Draper, Utah, Ephraim Hanks Recollections. In the fall of 1856, I spent considerable of my time fishing in Utah Lake; and in traveling backward and forward between that lake and Salt Lake City. I had occasion to stop once overnight with Gurnsey Brown[45], in

---

[44] Solomon Kimball, A King of Western Scouts, Improvement Era, Vol XVIII, February, 1915, pp. 211-12.

[45] Joseph Gurnsey Brown was born November 8, 1824 at Dryden, New York. His father, Ebenezer, married a widow Phebe Draper Palmer, who had a large family. Both Ebenezer and Phebe were enlisted in the Mormon Battalion in 1846 and therefore, left Gurnsey, age 22, and his sister Harriet, and her husband Oliver Stratton, with the responsibility of bringing the family across the plains. They met their father and mother in Salt Lake in 1849.

Ebenezer and his family took up land south of Salt Lake City on what was called Willow Creek, but later named Draper. They built the first house in Draper in 1850. On December 31, 1851, Gurnsey married 16 year old Harriet Maria Young, the only daughter

Draper, about nineteen miles south of Salt Lake City. Being somewhat fatigued after the day's journey, I retired to rest quite early, and while I still lay wide awake in my bed I heard a voice calling me by name, and then saying: "The handcart people are in trouble and you are wanted; will you go and help them?" I turned instinctively in the direction from whence the voice came and beheld an ordinary-sized man in the room. Without hesitation I answered, "Yes, I will go if I am called." I then turned around to go to sleep, but had laid only a few minutes when the voice called a second time, repeating almost the same words as on the first occasion. My answer was the same as before. This was repeated a third time. When I got up the next morning I says to Brother Brown, "The hand-cart people are in trouble, and I have promised to go out and help them," but I did not tell him of my experiences during the night. I now hastened to Salt Lake City.

Sunday, October 26, 1856, Salt Lake City, Tabernacle, Journal History. Two meetings were held in the Tabernacle. Pres. Heber C. Kimball spoke in the forenoon. He asked for 10 teams to volunteer to go and help the handcart

---

of Lorenzo Dow and Persis Young. In 1856 he was asked to take provisions to the belated handcart companies of saints who were struggling to reach the Valley before winter. Among those that Gurnsey brought back to the Valley were two young ladies from the Hunt Company, Esther Brown and Elizabeth White. Both Esther and Elizabeth were taken to Draper to stay with Gurnsey and his wife Harriet. Later Gurnsey married Esther Brown and Elizabeth married Isaac M. Stewart of Draper on March 8th, 1857. Isaac Stewart served as the first bishop of Draper until his death in 1890 or for a period of 34 years. Their home still stands as a landmark in Draper.

Gurnsey was later called on a mission to the "Muddy" and then reassigned to Kanab. There he spent the rest of his years until he passed away in 1907.

emigrants. About 120 persons volunteered to send teams.

Sunday, October 26, 1856, Salt Lake City, Tabernacle, Wilford Woodruff Journal. At the close of [President Kimball's] remarks He called for all the Horse teams in the City & Country to go into the Mountains & pick up the companies who were coming with Hand Carts & bring them into the City. 115 Teams were raised in a few moments. All were to be prepared to start in the morning.

Sunday, October 26, 1856, Salt Lake City, Tabernacle, Ephraim Hanks Recollections. I... arrived in Salt Lake City on the Saturday, preceding the Sunday [October 26th] on which the call was made for volunteers to go out and help the last hand-cart companies in. When some of the brethren responded by explaining that they could get ready to start in a few days, I spoke at once saying, "I am ready now!" The next day I was wending my way eastward over the mountains with a light wagon all alone.

November 1856, from South Pass to Cottonwood Creek, Ephraim Hanks Recollections.[46] The terrific storm which caused the immigrants so much suffering and loss overtook me near the South Pass, where I stopped about three days with Redick N. Allred, who had come out with provisions for the immigrants. The storm during these three days was simply awful. In all my travels in the Rocky Mountains both before and afterwards, I have seen no worse. When at length the snow ceased falling, it lay on the ground so deep that for many days it was impossible to move wagons through it.

Being deeply concerned about the possible fate of the

---

[46] Andrew Jenson, The Contributor, February, 1893, vol. XIL, pp. 202-205.

immigrants, and feeling anxious to learn of their condition, I determined to start out on horseback to meet them; and for this purpose I secured a pack-saddle and two animals (one to ride and one to pack), from Brother Allred, and began to make my way slowly through the snow alone. After traveling for some time I met Joseph A. Young and one of the Garr boys, two of the relief company which had been sent from Salt Lake City to help the companies. They had met the immigrants and were now returning with important dispatches from the camps to the headquarters of the Church, reporting the awful condition of the companies.

In the meantime I continued my lonely journey, and the night after meeting Elders Young and Garr, I camped in the snow in the mountains. As I was preparing to make a bed in the snow with the few articles that my pack animal carried for me, I thought how comfortable a buffalo robe would be on such an occasion, and also how I could relish a little buffalo meat for supper, and before lying down for the night I was instinctively led to ask the Lord to send me a buffalo. Now, I am a firm believer in the efficacy of prayer, for I have on many different occasions asked the Lord for blessings, which He in His mercy has bestowed on me. But when I after praying as I did on that lonely night in the South Pass, looked around me and spied a buffalo bull within fifty yards of my camp, my surprise was complete; I had certainly not expected so immediate an answer to my prayer. However, I soon collected myself and was not at a loss to know what to do. Taking deliberate aim at the animal, my first shot brought him down; he made a few jumps only, and then rolled down into the very hollow where I was encamped. I was soon busily engaged skinning my game, finishing which, I spread the hide on the snow and placed my bed upon it. I next prepared supper, eating tongue and other choice parts of the animal I had killed, to my heart's content. After this I enjoyed a refreshing night's sleep, while my horses were browsing on the sage brush.

Early the next morning I was on my way again, and soon reached what is known as the Ice Springs Bench. There I happened upon a herd of buffalo, and killed a nice cow. I was impressed to do this, although I did not know why until a few hours later, but the thought occurred to my mind that the hand of the Lord was in it, as it was a rare thing to find buffalo herds around that place at this late part of the season. I skinned and dressed the cow; then cut up part of its meat in long strips and loaded my horses with it. Thereupon I resumed my journey, and traveled on till towards evening. I think the sun was about an hour high in the west when I spied something in the distance that looked like a black streak in the snow. As I got near to it, I perceived it moved; then I was satisfied that this was the long looked for hand-cart company, led by Captain Edward Martin. I reached the ill-fated train just as the immigrants were camping for the night. The sight that met my gaze as I entered their camp can never be erased from my memory. The starved forms and haggard countenances of the poor sufferers, as they moved about slowly, shivering with cold, to prepare their scanty evening meal was enough to touch the stoutest heart. When they saw me coming, they hailed me with joy inexpressible, and when they further beheld the supply of fresh meat I brought into camp, their gratitude knew no bounds. Flocking around me, one would say, "Oh, please, give me a small peace of meat;" another would exclaim, "My poor children are starving, do give me a little;" and children with tears in their eyes would call out, "Give me some, give me some." At first I tried to wait on them and handed out the meat as they called for it; but finally I told them to help themselves. Five minutes later both my horses had been released of their extra burden--the meat was all gone, and the next few hours found the people in camp busily engaged in cooking and eating it, with thankful hearts.

A prophecy had been made by one of the brethren that

the company should feast on buffalo meat when their provisions might run short; my arrival in their camp, loaded with meat, was the beginning of the fulfillment of that prediction; but only the beginning, for them as we journeyed along.

When I saw the terrible condition of the immigrants on first entering their camp, my heart almost melted within me. I rose up in my saddle and tried to speak cheering and comforting words to them. I told them also that they should all have the privilege to ride into Salt Lake City, as more teams were coming.

After dark, on the evening of my arrival in the hand-cart camp, a woman passed the camp fire where I was sitting crying aloud. Wondering what was the matter, my natural impulse led me to follow her. She went straight to Daniel Tyler's wagon, where she told the heartrending story of her husband being at the point of death, and in pleading tones she asked Elder Tyler to come and administer to him. This good brother, tired and weary as he was, after pulling hand-carts all day, had just retired for the night, and was a little reluctant in getting up; but on this earnest solicitation he soon arose, and we both followed the woman to the tent, in which we found the apparently lifeless form of her husband. On seeing him, Elder Tyler remarked, "I cannot administer to a dead man." Brother Tyler requested me to stay and lay out the supposed dead brother, while he returned to his wagon to seek that rest which he needed so much. I immediately stepped back to the camp fire where several of the brethren were sitting and addressing myself to Elders Grant, Kimball and one or two others, I said, "Will you boys do just as I tell you?" The answer was in the affirmative. We then went to work and built a fire near the tent which I and Elder Tyler had just visited. Next we warmed some water, and washed the dying man whose name was Blair, from head to foot. I then anointed him with consecrated oil over his whole body, after which we laid hands on him and

126

commanded him in the name of Jesus Christ to breathe and live. The effect was instantaneous. For the man who was dead to all appearances immediately began to breathe, sat up in his bed and commenced to sing a hymn. His wife unable to control her feelings of joy and thankfulness ran through the camp exclaiming: "My husband was dead but is now alive praise be the name of God. The man who brought the buffalo meat has healed him."

This circumstance caused a great general excitement in the whole camp and many of the drooping spirits began to take fresh courage from that very hour. After this the greater portion of my time was devoted to waiting on the sick. "Come to me, help me, please administer to my sick wife, or my dying child," were some of the requests that were being made of me almost hourly for some time after I had joined the emigrants, and I spent days going from tent to tent administering to the sick. Truly the Lord was with me and others of his servants who labored faithfully together with me in that day of trial and suffering. The result of this, our labor of love certainly redounded to the honor and glory of a kind and merciful God. In scores of instances when we administered to the sick and rebuked the diseases in the name of the Lord Jesus Christ, the sufferers would rally at once: they were healed almost instantly. I administered to many each day and to scores during the journey and many of the lives were saved by the power of God....

I have but a very little to say about the sufferings of Captain Martin's company before I joined it; but it had passed through terrible ordeals. Women and the larger children helped the men to pull the hand-carts, and in crossing the frozen streams, they had to break the ice with their feet. In fording the Platte River, the largest stream they had to cross after the cold weather set in, the clothes of the immigrants were frozen stiff around their bodies before they could exchange them for others. This is supposed to have been the cause of the many deaths which occurred soon afterwards. It has been stated on good authority that nineteen immigrants died one night. The survivors who performed the last acts of kindness to those who perished, were not strong enough to dig the graves of sufficient depth to preserve the bodies from the wild beasts, and wolves were actually seen tearing open the graves before the company was out of sight. Many of the survivors, in witnessing the terrible afflictions and loses, became at last almost stupefied or mentally dazed, and did not seem to realize the terrible condition they were in. The suffering from the lack of sufficient food also told on the people. When the first relief teams met the immigrants, there was only one day's quarter rations left in camp.

Martin Handcart Company, 1856

November 1856, from Martin's Cove to Cottonwood Creek, Martin Company, John Jaques Journal. At length, preparations having been completed for a final start from Devil's Gate and vicinity, the handcart company left the ravine. The precise date I cannot give, but I think it must have been about the 10th of November. I cannot remember the handcarts after leaving the ravine and my impression is that none were taken from there.[47] Be that as it may, by this time there was a sufficiency of wagons to take in most if not all of the baggage of the company, and to carry some of the people. It was a trying time that day in leaving the ravine. One perplexing difficulty was to determine who should ride, for many must still walk, though, so far as I recollect, and certainly for most of the company, the cart occupation was

---

[47] According to the Journal History, some persons of the company recalled that a few carts were taken along several days longer.

gone. There was considerable crying of women and children, and perhaps a few of the men, whom the wagons could not accommodate with a ride. One of the relief party remarked that in all the mobbings and drivings of the Mormons he had seen nothing like it. C.H. Wheelock could scarcely refrain from shedding tears, and he declared that he would willingly give his own life if that would save the lives of the emigrants. After a time a start was effected and the march was recommenced along the valley of the Sweetwater toward the setting sun....

So the company slowly, not altogether as they had at first, but strung out in a long line that made a needle and trailing black line in the snow. No one sang, no one talked. Folks just pushed along at their own pace and tried not to think of how the days and nights stretch into weeks and months before the last of them found a long sleep in a trench of snow.

While on the Sweetwater, Eph Hanks was met one day. He had left his wagon behind him and came on alone on horseback and had managed to kill a buffalo. Some others of the relief parties, further this way [towards Salt Lake City], had come to the conclusion that the rear companies of the emigration had perished in the snow, but Eph was determined to go along, even alone, and see for himself. Wm. H. Kimball left Salt Lake again, Nov. 11th, with Hosea Stout, James Ferguson, and Joseph Simmons, and met the handcart company four miles beyond the first station on the Sweetwater, but I forget where that was. By this time the shoes of many of the emigrants had "given out", and that was no journey for shoeless men, women and children to make at such a season of the year, and trudge it on foot.

And [at] evening, just before sunset, a strange quiver like a thrill of hopefulness was communicated down the wavering line. Coming toward the train was a lone man leading two horses with great pieces of buffalo hung on each side of the animals.

129

It was Brother Ephraim Hanks and he had brought fresh buffalo meat that everyone set to cooking at his own fire. But more than meat, he brought them hope, the advance scouts of the rescue party were just a day away, and behind them a day or two further down the road were food and clothing and a chance to rest.

"It was like this," he was saying, his large hands spread out to the fire. "No matter what I did or where I went I couldn't forget you folks. I kept wondering how you were getting on, what with the early snows and everything."

"This night I was down near Utah Lake where I had gone fishing.... I was after a load that time, not just a string for supper. Well, I was staying at Gurnsey Brown's place, and though the bed was comfortable enough, I could not sleep. Finally I did drop off, but no sooner than I'd done it I was waked up again. Somebody said, 'Ephraim!' That's my name, so I said, 'Yes?'

"But it wasn't Gurnsey that was speaking. No one was in the room. Then my name was spoken again. My heart was like to pound right out of my body, but I couldn't see anything. Third time the voice said 'Ephraim,' seemed like it was sort of sharp and out of patience.

"I said, 'Yes, yes. Is there something I can do for you?' Then the voice said clear as if I'd been face to face with a neighbor, 'Ephraim, that handcart company is in trouble, will you help them out?'

"I got right out of bed. Gurnsey, he got my team hooked up and Sister Brown fixed me a bite and some food to carry along. Got to Salt Lake about daylight, and what should happen but I met a messenger from brother Brigham, on his way to fetch me....

"Seems since I was a boy that the Lord has always been willing to keep in touch with me if I'd keep in touch with Him.... This is the way I have it figured.... The Lord isn't going to fool around with any gifts just to impress folks. I don't hold for goings on in meetings like I've seen in some sects. I do know when a body needs the Lord--needs something the Lord can do for him so bad that there isn't any other way out--that is the time that the Lord will show His face or His voice and there'll be healings and tongues and prophesy and all the rest."

For a time no one spoke, then Brother Hanks said in a different, more jovial voice, "Yes, the Lord does some strange things, but I noticed he always counts on human folks to help Him out. Now I've traveled this road time and time again and at this time of year I wouldn't ever have expected to meet a buffalo. But you folks needed meat and he was put in my way. Now, if I hadn't been there, or if I couldn't have brought him down--well, the way I figure it, the Lord wouldn't have bothered to have him there, that's all...."

The next morning everyone in camp was talking about Brother Hanks, about his prayers for the sick, but even more the operations he had performed with his hunting knife. Many of the Saints were carrying frozen limbs which were endangering their lives. Brother Hanks anointed these folks and prayed that the amputation could be done without pain. Then when he took out his great hunting knife, held it to the fire to cleanse it, and took off the dying limb with its keen blade; many with tears in their eyes said they hadn't felt a thing.

November 1856, Cottonwood Creek, Martin Company, Isaac John Wardle Recollections.[48] At this time Ephraim Hanks came to their camp. [He] found them discouraged and most of them had given up. Their camp was without food and fuel. Hanks had killed 2 buffalo just before

---

[48] Recorded by his granddaughter, Ann Wardle Thompson Rupp.

they met [him]. Soon they were warm and eating of the fresh meat which was prepared by the women of the camp. [He] also told them that help was coming from Utah to meet them. On the Wyoming plains several of their members froze to death, as not only was their food scarce, but clothing was very poor, lots even without shoes and warm coats.

Tuesday, November 11, 1856, Cottonwood Creek, the Rescue Party with the Martin Company, Daniel W. Jones Account. I followed the train this day to their second encampment and the next day traveled with them. There was much suffering, deaths occurring often. Eph Hanks arrived in camp from the valley and word that some of the teams that had reached South Pass and should have met us here, had turned back towards home and tried to persuade Redick Allred, who was left there with a load of flour, to go back with them. The men who did this might have felt justified; they said it was no use going further, that we had doubtless all perished. I will not mention their names for it was always looked upon by the company as cowardly in the extreme. If this had not occurred, it was the intention of Capt. Grant to have sent someone down to us with a load of flour. As it was, by the time any was received, the people were in a starving condition, and could not spare it.

CHAPTER 4
CROSSINGS OF THE SWEETWATER

As the Trail followed the Sweetwater River, it was necessary to make several crossings simply because of the topography of the land. Beginning with the first crossing near Independence Rock, the trail crosses the Sweetwater nine times. Some of these crossings were more significant than others.

One of the places remembered well by the pioneers was called **Three Crossings.** Along this section of the Sweetwater River, the easiest way to proceed was to cross the river three times. To the south of the river, about 1/4 of a mile, was the Three Crossings Pony Express and Telegraph Station. The station was burned by Indians in 1861. The last message from the telegrapher to St. Joseph, Missouri stated, "Indians have the Three Crossing's surrounded--it is burning--all the men are killed--I am wounded--we have buried the gold and silver in a Dutch oven"--the message ceased. The surrounding terrain dictated the three crossings. Because the Sweetwater wriggles snakelike between granite hills on one side and deep and impassable sand patches on the other, the overlanders were obliged to take a laborious course. The wagons passed from the south to the north side at the first crossing, and a mile further upstream crossed back to the south bank again. Almost immediately a third crossing was made again to the north bank, and after traveling along a narrow bank or in the bed of the stream, if the water was low, the wagons emerged from the gap onto a broad flat.[49] William Clayton's Emigrant Guide, published in 1848, described the area as follows: "ROAD ARRIVES AT THE RIVER. Leave the old road and ford the

---

[49] Paul C. Henderson, Landmarks on the Oregon Trail.

river. By fording here, the road is shorter, and you avoid rough very heavy, sandy road. ROAD TURNS BETWEEN THE ROCKY RIDGES. After this, you ford the river twice-- but it is easily forded. Then the road leaves the river again."

The next crossing is known as the **Fifth Crossing of the Sweetwater.** Clayton's Emigrant Guide also describes that location: "FIFTH CROSSING--GOOD CAMPING PLACE. After this, the road leaves the river again, and you will probably find no water fit to drink for sixteen and a half miles."

Past the Fifth Crossing, the trail passes a swampy area that is called **Ice Spring.** Clayton's Emigrant Guide describes the area: "On the top of this (reaching the bluff after leaving the Sweetwater), we appear to have a level road where there is plenty of grass and apparently swampy and soft. It extends in the same direction with the road a mile and a half and appears to terminate where the road crosses the lower land although the grass and hollow continue southward for some distance. Just above where the road crosses at the west end there is some water standing around a small, circular, swampy spot of land probably about a half an acre. Near the edge at the northwest corner is a hole dug which is called the Ice Spring. The water in the hole smells strong of sulphur and alkali and is not pleasant tasting, but under the water, over a foot deep, there is as clear ice as I every saw and good tasting. Some of the brethren had broken some pieces off which floated and I ate some of it which tasted sweet and pleasant. The ice is said to be four inches thick."

Sixteen miles beyond the Fifth Crossing, past Ice Spring, the emigrants came to the **Sixth Crossing** of the Sweetwater. It was here that the main Rescue Party found the Willie Company on October 21, 1856.

The **Last Crossing** of the Sweetwater does not occur until after the trail passes Rock Creek, at a location known as the **Burnt Ranch**, just before **South Pass.** (Events occurring at the Last Crossing, Burnt Ranch, South Pass and beyond are discussed in the last chapter.)

1847 Pioneer Company

Thursday, June 24, 1847, Fifth Crossing, William Clayton. Morning fine but cool. It was calculated to make an early start so as to pass the two companies of the Missourians and get the best chance for feed at night, but they started out a half an hour before we were ready. We proceeded onward at 6:15 and a little over a mile from where we camped, found the river again bending northwest while the road continues near a west course and soon rises a high bluff [Ice Spring Bench].

Thursday, June 24, 1847, Ice Spring, Pioneer Company, Wilford Woodruff Journal. We traveled today 5 miles and came to the frozen or ice spring and stopped and examined it. I found the spring to be strongly impregnated with sulphur, so much so that it could not be drank. The water would boil up out of a crevasse, a piece of bog, yet all around it, it was so cold, that after removing the turf about 6 inches, a solid body of ice was found about 14 inches thick, some of it, we got up with an axe and spades. Near this was a small pond of... salt and sulphur and something seemed to be in the bog.

Thursday, June 24, 1847, Sixth Crossing, Pioneer Company, William Clayton. After traveling from the ice spring ten and a quarter miles over a very uneven road, we descended a very steep bluff close in the rear of one of the Missourian Companies. The other had halted a few miles ahead and we passed by them. While winding around and

135

descending from this bluff we came in sight of the river again [Sixth Crossing] and about the same time, Elder Kimball picked up an Indian arrow point made of flint stone and nearly perfect. It was almost as white as alabaster. At 3:30 we tarried a little south from the road and formed our encampment in a line so as to enclose a bend in the river, having traveled seventeen and three-quarters miles without halting on account of there being no water fit for cattle to drink. The feed here is very good and plenty of willow bushes for fuel. The river is about three rods wide and clearer and very cold. The last five or six miles of the road were not so sandy but hard and good traveling. One of the Missourian companies have gone on, but the other camped a piece down the river at the fording place. A while before dark when the brethren were fetching up their teams, John Holman, while bringing up Presidents Young's best horse, having his loaded rifle in his hand, the horse undertook to run back past him and to prevent his running back, he jammed his gun at him. The cock caught in his clothes, the gun went off, lodging the ball in the animal's body. It entered a little forward of the right hind leg on the under side of his belly making quite a large hole. The horse walked to camp but it is the opinion of many he cannot survive long. He appears to be in great pain, the sweat falling from his forehead in large drops. President Young is evidently filled with deep sorrow on account of this accident but attaches no blame to John who seems very grieved. The brethren generally feel sorrowful, this being the second horse shot by accident on this mission.

Friday, June 25, 1847, Sixth Crossing, Pioneer Company, William Clayton. President Young's horse is dead. The morning is fine but very cool. At twenty minutes to seven o'clock, we pursued our journey fording the river a quarter of a mile below where we left the road last night. We found it still nearly three feet deep and the current very swift.

136

After proceeding a half a mile beyond the ford, we crossed a stream about a rod wide which appears to come from the northeast and empties into the river a little farther up.

Willie Handcart Company, 1856

Friday, October 17, 1856, Three Crossings, Willie Company, William Woodward, Clerk. William Philpot, aged 51 years, from Southampton, Hampshire, England died this morning about 2 o'clock. Camp rolled on in the morning, roads good, forded the Sweetwater & nooned, after travelling over 7 miles. Bro. Findlay found an ox able to work. A calf gave out & was killed by wolves. The company rolled on again, forded the Sweetwater twice between the mountains & travelled on a piece & camped; willows plenty for fuel; travelled about 13 miles through the day.

Saturday, October 18, 1856, Fifth Crossing, Willie Company, John Chislett Journal. We travelled on in misery and sorrow day after day. Sometimes we made a pretty good distance, but at other times we were only able to make a few miles' progress. Finally we were overtaken by a snow storm which the shrill wind blew furiously about us. The snow fell several inches deep, as we travelled along, but we dared not stop, for we had a sixteen-mile journey to make, and short of it we could not get wood and water.[50]

Sunday, October 19, 1856, Fifth Crossing, Willie Company, Joseph B. Elder Journal. It was at the commencement of the 16 mile drive without water that we gave

---

[50] Emigrants were probably accustomed to using William Clayton's Emigrant Guide, which states: "after this... you will probably find no water fit to drink for sixteen and a half miles."

out the last of the flour we was then 28 miles below rocky ridge [16 miles to the Sixth Crossing and then an additional 12 miles to the bottom of Rocky Ridge] which made it about 50 miles to the South Pass and we had not yet herd whether there was any help coming to meet us or not but we were determined to do all we could. That day about noon there came up a snow storm it blew directly in our faces. The company that was ahead with the carts stopped and sheltered themselves from the storm. I was driving the foremost waggin. It was severe for the people was weak having been on short rations   I determined to keep ahead until I overtook the carts anyhow but by the time we caught up with the carts the clouds dispersed and the sun shone out and as we looked ahead Lo and behold we saw a waggin coming [the Express] and it was close such a shout as was raised in camp I never before herd it came from the hearts of faithful saints who felt that their lives was in the hands of their God but what made them shout was it meerly the sight of a waggin for we had met waggins before   no but it was that the spirit of the Lord bore testimony that they were saviors coming to their relief   and truly it was it was Brothers S. Wheelock   Jos. Young and 2 others   they brought us glorious news they had been to Zion and were returning with many of their brethren with teams and provisions to help us through.

Sunday, October 19, 1856, Fifth Crossing, Willie Company, Rowley Family History. On Sunday, 19 October, the handcarts rolled on. The weather was intensely cold and the first snow fell, though it did not begin to accumulate until the following morning. However, the lightly clad emigrants suffered severely. On that day, this important entry appears in the company diary: "Rolled on in the morning, weather very cold. Ann Rowley died this morning, aged 2 years. Some of the children were crying with cold." The reference in this entry to Ann Rowley is an error. We know that Ann Rowley

138

did not die on the plains. She arrived in Zion and lived to an old age. No other person in the company was listed with the same name. There were no other Rowley children besides Ann's. It is likely that the reported death was Eliza Rowley, age 33, Ann's stepdaughter.... Eliza Rowley traveled from Liverpool to Iowa City, then walked nearly a thousand miles before she succumbed to hunger, cold, and exhaustion. She died only hours before help arrived. When we celebrate the martyrs to the cause of truth in the eternities, we do not doubt that Eliza Rowley will stand tall among them. God bless us to remember her sacrifice, that we may be willing to do likewise.

Sunday, October 19, 1856, from Fifth Crossing to Sixth Crossing, Willie Company, William Woodward, Clerk. Rolled on in the morning, weather very cold. Ann Rowley died this morning, aged 2 years. Some of the children were crying with cold. Passed "Ice Springs"; just after we were past the "springs" a snow storm came on, which lasted for about half an hour. The company rolled on again, & were soon met by [the Express sent by the First Rescue Party] Cyrus H. Wheelock & Joseph A. Young & two other brethren from the Valley, bringing us the information that supplies were near at hand, the camp halted, a meeting was called. Brother Wheelock informed us of the liberality of the Saints in the Valley, of Bro. Brigham Young's kindheartedness in speaking in behalf of the Handcart Companies now on the plains, & of himself fitting up ten teams & wagons & supplying them with flour, &c. & others in proportion. During the day Eliza Smith, from Eldersfield, Worcestershire, England, aged 40 years died; also John Kockles, from Norwich, Norfolk, England, died; also, Daniel Osborn, from Norwich, Norfolk, England died; also Rasmus Hansen, from Falster, Denmark, died. Travelled thro' the day about 16 miles; camped at dark on the banks of the Sweetwater. The teams mistook the road & did not get into camp till around 10 p.m. [Note: The following additional notes were added to the diary after it was first prepared, presumably by William Woodward.]   C.H. Wheelock and Joseph A. Young with 2 other brethren [Stephen Taylor and Abel Garr] met us a short distance west of "Ice Springs" and brought us the cheering intelligence that assistance was near at hand; that several wagons loaded with flour, onions, and clothing including bedding was within a day's drive of us. That same night we issued all provisions to the camp, which was hard bread that was bought at Laramie (the last of our flour being issued the night before) left us about destitute of provisions for the camp.[51]

Sunday, October 19, 1856, from Fifth Crossing to Sixth Crossing, Willie Company, Levi Savage Journal. Fifth Crossing of the Sweetwater. At half past ten o'clock we started. In about one hour we encountered a very severely cold and blustering snowstorm. It lasted for one hour. The poorly clad women and children suffered much. At twelve o'clock we met Brother Wheelock and company who have come to our relief. He reported forty wagon loads of flour one day in advance of us. This was joyful news to us for we had eaten the last pound of flour, having only six small beefs and 400 pounds of biscuits to provision over 400 people. After a short meeting in which Brothers Wheelock and J. Young spoke cheeringly to the Saints, we moved on. The wind continued strong and cold. The children, the aged, and infirm fell back to the wagons until they were so full that all in them were extremely uncomfortable. Brother Kockles, aged 66 years, died during the day in a handcart hitched behind one of the wagons. Sister Smith and Daniel Osborn, age eight years, died in the wagons. They had been ill for some time. The carts

---

[51] The Jens Pederson Journal concurs that "the last flour was used on October 19th and that night the first snow fell".

140

arrived at the river at dark. One wagon, it being dark, took another road[52] and did not get into camp until eleven o'clock p.m. They were nearly exhausted and so were myself and teamsters.

Sunday, October 19, 1856, from Fifth Crossing to Sixth Crossing, Willie Company, John Chislett Journal. As we were resting for a short time at noon a light wagon was driven into our camp from the west. Its occupants were Joseph A. Young and Stephen Taylor. They informed us that a train of supplies was on the way, and we might expect to meet it in a day or two. More welcome messengers never came from the courts of glory than these two young men were to us. They lost no time after encouraging us all they could to press forward, but sped on further east to convey their glad news to Edward Martin and the fifth handcart company who left Florence about two weeks after us, and who it was feared were even worse off than we were. As they went from our view, many a hearty 'God bless you' followed them.

We pursued our journey with renewed hope and after untold toil and fatigue, doubling teams frequently, going back to fetch up the straggling carts, and encouraging those who had dropped by the way to a little more exertion in view of our soon-to-be improved condition, we finally, late at night, got all to camp--the wind howling frightfully and the snow eddying around us in fitful gusts. But we had found a good camp among the willows, and after warming and partially drying

---

[52] This was probably the "Seminoe Cut-off" which was opened in 1854. It by-passed the 7th and 8th crossings of the Sweetwater as well as Rocky Ridge. It was on the south side of the Sweetwater River and converged with the main trail at the Ninth or Last Crossing of the Sweetwater. The main problem with this cut-off as well as some of the others, i.e. Sublette or Greenwood Cut-off, was the lack of water and feed for animals.

ourselves before good fires, we ate our scanty fare, paid our usual devotions to the Deity and retired to rest with hopes of coming aid.

The morning before the storm, or rather, the morning of the day on which it came, we issued the last ration of flour. On this fatal morning, therefore, we had none to issue. We had, however, a barrel or two of hard bread which Captain Willie had procured at Fort Laramie in view of our destitution. This was equally and fairly divided among all the company. Two of our poor broken-down cattle were killed and their carcasses issued for beef. With this we were informed that we would have to subsist until the coming supplies reached us. All that now remained in our commissary were a few pounds each of sugar and dried applies, about a quarter of a sack of rice and a small quantity (possibly 20 or 25 lbs.) of hard bread. The brother who had been our commissary all the way from Liverpool had not latterly acted in a way to merit the confidence of the company; but it is hard to handle the provisions and suffer hunger at the same time, so I will not write a word of condemnation. These few scanty supplies were on this memorable morning turned over to me by Captain Willie, with strict injunctions to distribute them only to the sick and to mothers for their hungry children, and even to them in as sparing a manner as possible. It was an unenviable place to occupy, a hard duty to perform; but I acted to the best of my ability, using all the discretion I could.

Sunday, October 19, 1856, Sixth Crossing near Sweetwater Station, Willie Company, George Cunningham Journal. Our Captain intended to keep his word, and commenced to kill off the cattle but they were nearly as poor as we were. We used to boil the bones and drink the soup and eat what little meat there was. We greedily devoured the hides also. I myself had took a piece of hide when I could get it, scorched off hair, roasted it a little on the coals, cut it into little pieces so that I could swallow it and bolted it down my throat for supper and thought it was most delicious. Many were frozen to death. I think that there were only five or six men in camp towards the last but what were frozen. Our Captain drove all he could and did his duty. He was badly frozen and came very close to dying. Some would sacrifice themselves by giving their food or perhaps some old blanket that covered them. In common cares, we cannot tell what our friends and neighbors are, but there are circumstances which undoubtedly proved them.

October, 1856, along the Sweetwater River, Willie Company, John Chislett Journal. Life went out as smoothly as a lamp ceases to burn when the oil is gone. At first, the deaths occurred slowly and irregularly, but in a few days, at more frequent intervals, until we soon thought it unusual too leave a campground without burying one or more persons.... Every death weakened our forces. In my hundred I could not raise enough men to pitch a tent when we camped.... I wonder I did not die, as many did who were stronger than I was.... We traveled on in misery and sorrow.

October, 1856, Sixth Crossing and vicinity, Willie Company, History of William James. It was not uncommon to take the clothing from the dead to cover the living. Many lives were saved in this way. Storm after storm swept over the company. The Saints became numb and apathetic. Most lost the desire to live and in many cases lay down to stay. To add to this misery, a heavy snow storm caught them at the last crossing of the Sweetwater. Sarah James, who had just turned 18 in August, tells this story: "We were cold all the time. It was either rain or snow or wind. Even when you were wrapped up in a blanket your teeth chattered. Father told us one night that the flour was gone and that the word was that we might not get help for some time. Father was white and drawn. I knew that Mother was worried about him, for he was getting weaker all the time and seemed to feel that there was no use in all the struggle. Mother had taken as much of the load off his shoulders as she could in pulling the cart. We girls and Rueben did most of the work so Father could rest a lot. Mother didn't have much to say, and I wondered if she remembered that council meeting in Camp Iowa and wished that we had taken the advise of the more experienced people. I am sure that many of us had those thoughts.

"We were grateful one morning when we heard that the Captain had ordered all the animals in the company killed so that we could have fresh meat. We were so hungry that we didn't stop to think what it would do for our wagons. How good the soup tasted made from the bones of those cows although there wasn't any fat on them. The hides we used to roast after taking all the hair off of it. I even decided to cook the tatters of my shoes and make soup of them. It brought a smile to my Father's sad face when I made the suggestion, but Mother was a bit impatient with me and told me that I would have to eat the muddy things myself.

"It snowed day after day, and we managed to get a few miles each day. We were sort of dizzy and sleeping a lot of the time, so I can't remember too well just what did happen all of the time. Sometimes when we felt that we just had to rest for a time, a Captain would come up and help us pull our cart for a time. I am sure we would have laid down and died if it hadn't been for their help and encouragement. Sometimes they had to get cross with some people. I can remember the time when one of the men who was pulling a cart just ahead of us laid down in his shafts and started to cry. We all wanted to cry with him. One of the Captains, I don't remember just who, came up to him and just slapped him in the face. Then the man was so made that he jumped right up and started to run with his cart. I remember that it was a mean way to treat the poor fellow but now, that it saved his life....

144

"The time came when we were all too tired to move, so we huddled in our covers, close to each other for warmth. It was snowing and we were so tired. Suddenly we heard a shout, and through the swirling snow we saw men, wagons and mules coming towards us. Slowly we had realized that help had come. The wagons brought food and clothing. They hauled in wood for us, and as we gathered around the huge fire and ate the delicious morsels of food, we came alive enough to thank the Lord for his mercy to us.

"We heard later that one of the missionary groups who had stopped over with us on their way home from the East had finally got word to the Valley that there were companies on the plains who were starving and by now freezing to death. Word came to Brigham Young during October conference. He called the Saints together and instead of sermons he gave orders that they were to get help to the needy now.... Father Willy and another brother had gone out to find help and nearly missed the rescue trains in the blinding snow.

"Now that we had food and warmth for our bodies, we realized that we would have to move on for the weather was getting worse as the days went on. It was decided that we would leave everything except some extra clothing, utensils to cook in and many of our carts which would be guarded until they could be brought on in the Spring. Those who couldn't walk would ride in the wagons and we would travel as fast as we could to the Valley. I remember the rest of the journey as being terrible with cold and snow but we did have food and some hope of getting to Zion."

Monday, October 20, 1856, Sixth Crossing, Willie Company, William Woodward, Clerk. Monday, 20 October. This morning there was about 4 inches of snow on the ground. Anna F. Tait from Glasgow, Scotland, aged 31 years died; Capt. Willie & Joseph Elder left camp to meet the "Relief Train" that had been sent from the Valley. Our provisions were all issued last night & that was hard bread. [Note: The following additional notes were apparently added to the diary after the initial entry, both portions of the entry presumably were made by William Woodward, the last clerk of the company.] In the morning we found the ground covered with snow 4 or 5 inches deep. Bro. Willie and Joseph Elder started in search of the "Relief Train" as we could not move our camp and they did not arrive back again till the following evening, when the "Relief Train" under the charge of George D. Grant came to our camp. Flour and onions were issued that same evening, clothing, bedding, etc. were given to the camp the next morning. 9 persons were buried at that camping ground. Snow was on the ground and looked dismal. W.H. Kimball and others with 6 wagons went with us to the Valley. G.D.Grant and others went on their way to meet the rear handcart companies. Crossing the Rocky Ridge was a severe and disastrous day to have. The weather was cold and it snowed and blowed, some of the time making it bad for the sick who rode in the wagons and for those who pulled the handcarts. The next day we buried 13 souls near Willow Creek on the banks of the Sweetwater.

Monday, October 20, 1856, Sixth Crossing, Willie Company, Levi Savage Journal. Sixth Crossing of the Sweetwater. This morning when we arose, we found several inches of snow on the ground and it is yet snowing. The cattle and people are so much reduced with short food and hard work that except we get assistance, we surely cannot move far in this snow. Brothers Willie and Elder started on horseback about ten o'clock to search for the wagons that Wheelock reported a short distance in our advance. This morning we issued the last bread, or breadstuffs, in our possession. It continued snowing severely during the day. We expected Brother Willie would return this evening, but he has not come.

Monday, October 20, 1856, Sixth Crossing, Willie Company, Joseph B. Elder Journal. The next morning when we got up we found the snow about 6 or 8 inches deep   the camp was hungry naked and cold   to rush them into the snow would be certain death to a great many of them for we had not yet met the relief company only one waggin which had passed us and went on to the other company behind us [Martin Company] Brother Willy who was the captain of the company left the charge of the camp in the hands of Broth. Atwood and we started ahead in search of our brethren   we rode 12 miles where we expected to find them but they was not there   we ascended the rocky Ridge   the snow and an awful cold wind blew in our faces all day   we crossed the rocky ridge and upon the west bank of the North Fork of the Sweetwatter [probably a reference to Rock Creek] we found a friendly guide post which pointed us to their camp down upon the Sweetwatter in amongst the willows   when they saw us they raised a shout and ran out to meet us   great was their joy to hear from us for they had long been in search of us   they could scarcely give us time to tell our story they were so anxious to hear all about us   their camp being 27 miles from ours.

Monday, October 20, 1856, Sixth Crossing, Willie Company, John Chislett Journal. Being surrounded by snow a foot deep, out of provisions, many of our people sick, and our cattle dying, it was decided that we should remain in our present camp until the supply train reached us. It was also resolved in council that Captain Willie with one man [Joseph Elder] should go in search of the supply train and apprise its leader of our condition, and hasten him to our help. When this was done we settled down and made our camp as comfortable as we could. As Captain Willie and his companion left for the West, many a heart was lifted in prayer for their success and speedy return. They were absent three days [other journals suggest they were absent two days]--three days which I shall never forget. The scanty allowance of hard bread and poor beef, distributed as described, was mostly consumed the first day by the hungry, ravenous, famished souls.

We killed more cattle and issued the meat; but, eating it without bread, did not satisfy hunger, and to those who were suffering from dysentery it did more harm than good. This terrible disease increased rapidly amongst us during these three days, and several died from exhaustion. Before we renewed our journey the camp became so offensive and filthy that words would fail to describe its condition, and even common decency forbids the attempt. Suffice it to say that all the disgusting scenes which the reader might imagine would certainly not equal the terrible reality. It was enough to make the heavens weep. The recollection of it unmans me even now--those three days! During that time I visited the sick, the widows whose husbands died in serving them, and the aged who could not help themselves, to know for myself where to dispense the few articles that had been placed in my charge for distribution. Such craving hunger I never saw before, and may God in his mercy spare me the sight again.

Tuesday, October 21, 1856, Willow Creek to Sixth Crossing, Rescue Party locates Willie Company, Harvey Cluff Account. Preparations were made and early in the morning of the following day we were on the road pushing our way for Captain Willie's camp. The depth of snow made travelling extremely difficult and the whole day was spent before we reached camp. It was about sunset when we came in sight of the camp; which greatly resembled an Esqumeax [Eskimo] Village fully one mile away. The snow being a foot deep and paths having been made from tent to tent gave the camp that appearance. As we reached an eminence overlooking the camp, which was located on a sagebrush plain near the river a mile away. When the people of the camp sighted us approaching, they set up such a shout as to echo through the hills. Arriving within the confines of this emigrant camp a most thrilling and touching scene was enacted, melting to tears the stoutest hearts. Young maidens and feeble old ladies, threw off all the restraint and freely embraced their deliverers expressing in a flow of kisses, the gratitude which their tongues failed to utter. This was certainly the most timely arrival of a relief party recorded in history.... To give an idea of the critical condition of those people I will say that our camp was pitched about fifty yards from the tents of the emigrants and each meal was over in our camp and the bones and crumbs from our meals were thrown out on the snow, young men would gather them up and knaw and suck them as long as they gathered any substance.

Tuesday, October 21, 1856, Willow Creek to Sixth Crossing, Rescue Party locates Willie Company, Daniel W. Jones Account. We started immediately through the storm to reach Brother Willie's camp. On arriving we found them in a condition that would stir the feelings of the hardest heart. They were in a poor place, the storm having caught them where fuel was scarce. They were out of provisions and really freezing and starving to death. The morning after our arrival nine were buried in one grave. We did all we could to relieve them. The boys struck out on horseback and dragged up a lot of wood; provisions were distributed and all went to work to cheer the sufferers. Soon there was an improvement in camp, but many poor, faithful people had gone too far--had passed beyond the power to recruit. Our help came too late for some and many died after our arrival.

William Kimball with a few men and wagons turned back, taking the oversight of this company to help them in. Capt. Grant left a wagon load of flour near the Pass with Redick Allred to guard it. There were several hundred people with Brother Willie. They had a few teams, but most of them

149

had become too weak to be of much service. When we left Salt Lake it was understood that other teams would follow until all the help needed would be on the road. The greater portion of our company now continued towards Devil's Gate, traveling through snow all the way.

Tuesday, October 21, 1856, Sixth Crossing, Willie Company, William Woodward, Clerk. John Linford from Graveley, Cambridgeshire, England, aged 49 years died; also Richard Hardwick, from Moorhen's Cross, Herfordshire, England, aged 63 years; also Mary Ann Perkins, from Norwich, Norfolk, England, aged 62 years died; also Sophia Larsen from Lolland, Denmark, aged 11 years. Many children were crying for bread and the camp generally were destitute of food. A beef heifer was killed for the camp. Capt. Willie, Capt. Grant, W. H. Kimball & others with 14 wagons with horse & mule teams arrived in camp with flour, onions, & some clothing for the camp, this made the Saints feel well.

Tuesday, October 21, 1856, Sixth Crossing, Willie Company, John Chislett Journal. The storm which we encountered, our brethren from the Valley also met, and not knowing that we were utterly destitute, they encamped to await fine weather. But when Captain Willie found them and explained our real condition, they at once hitched up their teams and made all speed to come to our rescue. On the evening of the third [probably the second] day after Captain Willie's departure, just as the sun was sinking beautifully behind the distant hills, on an eminence immediately west of our camp several covered wagons, each drawn by four horses, were seen coming towards us. The news ran through the camp like wildfire, and all who were able to leave their beds turned out en masse to see them. A few minutes brought them sufficiently near to reveal our faithful captain slightly in advance of the train. Shouts of joy rent the air; strong men wept till tears ran freely down their furrowed and sun-burnt cheeks, and little children partook of the joy which some of them hardly understood, and fairly danced around with gladness. Restraint was set aside in the general rejoicing, and as the brethren entered our camp the sisters fell upon them and deluged the brethren with kisses. The brethren were so overcome that they could not for sometime utter a word, but in choking silence repressed all demonstration of those emotions that evidently mastered them. Soon, however, feeling was somewhat abated, and such a shaking of hands, such words of welcome, and such invocation of God's blessing have seldom been witnessed.

I was installed as regular commissary to the camp. The brethren turned over to me flour, potatoes, onions, and a limited supply of warm clothing for both sexes, besides quilts, blankets, buffalo-robes, woollen socks, etc. I first distributed the necessary provisions, and after supper divided the clothing, bedding, etc., where it was most needed. That evening, for the first time in quite a period, the songs of Zion were to be heard in the camp, and peals of laughter issued from the little knots of people as they chatted around the fires. The change seemed almost miraculous, so sudden was it from grave to gay, from sorrow to gladness, from mourning to rejoicing. With the cravings of hunger satisfied, and with hearts filled with gratitude to God and our good brethren, we all united in prayer, and then retired to rest.

Among the brethren who came to our succor were elders W.H. Kimball and G. D. Grant. They had remained but a few days in the Valley before starting back to meet us. May God ever bless them for their generous, unselfish kindness and their manly fortitude! They felt that they had, in a great measure, contributed to our sad position; but how nobly, how faithfully, how bravely they worked to bring us safely to the Valley--to the Zion of our hopes!

151

CHAPTER 5
ASCENDING ROCKY RIDGE

The second highest elevation[53] of the entire Mormon Trail is at **Rocky Ridge**, a climb that is more formidable than it first appears. Its name comes from the formation of layered rock that juts out from the ground at an angle and spans nearly the entire ridge. For much of the approximately five mile ascent, innumerable rocks and rock fragments make the trail extremely difficult.

William Clayton's Emigrant Guide describes the area as follows: "Road leaves the river. Good camping place. After this, the road winds around and over a succession of hills and hollows, for three miles. Rough, rocky ridges. Dangerous to wagons, and ought to be crossed with care."

The ascent up Rocky Ridge was especially treacherous for members of the Willie Company, who faced snow, ice, and extreme cold in addition to the rugged terrain. Many were frozen or died of exhaustion during the ascent. A memorial has been erected part way up the ridge, in recognition of those who lost their lives and of those who survived such extreme hardships there.

Past the summit of Rocky Ridge, the trail passes three small lakes or ponds known as **Lewiston Lakes**, and the trail proceeded to **Strawberry Creek**, a stream about five feet wide that was a good camping spot in warm weather.

---

[53] The Mormon Trail reaches its highest point near Aspen Ridge, west of Fort Bridger, Wyoming.

1847 Pioneer Company

June, 1847, Rocky Ridge, Pioneer Company, William Clayton. At 1:20 we proceeded again, our road running on the river banks two miles then turning to the northwest and ascending a succession of hills one after another for three miles farther, winding around and over hill and valley in some places over a good hard road, and in other places over rocks and broken fragments of rock, making it severe on wagons and requiring great care in teamsters. About a half mile north of the road at the top of this ridge there is a heavy bank of snow which some of the brethren went to visit and amused themselves by snowballing each other. Brother Carrington says there is every appearance of a rich lead mine in that place, having examined the place minutely.

June 1847, Rocky Ridge, Pioneer Company, Thomas Bullock. Leave this place at 1:30, continuing through the very narrow vale.... We ascended a long steep hill, finding many daisies which was a pleasant sight for me. Brother Wordsworth brought me a ball of snow which I ate; quite a treat for the Anniversary of my Wedding day.

June 1847, Rocky Ridge, Pioneer Company, Levi Jackman. This day we passed over some high hills. Some of them were covered with rock standing partly on the edge at an incline of about 45 degrees.

June 1847, Strawberry Creek, Pioneer Company, William Clayton. At 6:45 we formed our encampment on the north banks of a creek about five feet wide, having traveled this afternoon eleven and a half miles and during the day twenty and a quarter. This creek is very clear and cold. Its banks are well lined with willows and about a mile below the camp there is a grove of white poplar in which house logs may be obtained sixteen feet long and a foot through. There are several banks of snow a little to the north and some of the brethren have found ice, four or five inches thick and brought a quantity of it to camp. On the banks of the creek there are some groves of gooseberry bushes with small green berries on them. There are also some strawberry roots and flowers and a little white clover has been found, but there is yet no appearance of the great abundance of such things as travelers have represented. The land appears somewhat more likely to yield the nearer we approach to the mountains, but all calculations for farming in this region would be likely to fail on account of the scarcity of timber. It would only be natural to suppose that the nights are very cold here, while so much snow lies around. It requires considerable clothing to keep comfortable, but in the middle of the day it is equally hot. Some of the brethren have traveled up the banks of the Sweet Water river and represent it as tumbling and foaming over rocks and descending very rapidly on account of the great rise of the ground from noon halt to this place. They say it runs within a mile and a half south of this but it is probable it is only a branch of it as we are evidently not near the main branch yet. There is one of the gentile companies camped about a mile below, making the third company we have passed lately and it is the intention to keep ahead of them and have the advantage of the good feed and camping grounds.

June 1847, Strawberry Creek, Pioneer Company, George A. Smith. About half a mile below camp is a grove of quaking asps, covering five or six acres some of them from eight to ten inches in diameter.

Willie Handcart Company, 1856

Wednesday, October 22, 1856, Sixth Crossing to Bottom of Rocky Ridge, Willie Company, Levi Savage Journal. We prepared for starting and commenced moving about twelve o'clock. Brother Grant took a good portion of the teams and continued his journey to meet Brother Martin's company. Brother William Kimball took charge of our company. We traveled about ten miles and camped at the foot of what is called the Rock Ridge. I had charge of the teams. Because of their reduced strength and heavy loads, a large number of sick and children were in the wagons. I did not arrive in camp until late at night. The wind blew bleak and cold and firewood very scarce. The Saints were obliged to spread their light bedding on the snow, and in this cold state endeavored to obtain a little rest. Sister Philpot died about ten o'clock p.m., leaving two fatherless girls. Several others died during the night.

Thursday, October 23, 1856, Rocky Ridge, Willie Company, William Woodward, Clerk. Thursday, 23 October. Ascended a steep hill, traveled about 16 miles & camped on the Sweetwater. Crossed several creeks on the road, several men were near frozen thro the day; two teams loaded with sick did not get to camp till very late. James Gibbs from Leith, East Lothian, Scotland, aged 67 died; also Chesterton J. Gilman from Yarmouth, Suffolk England, aged 66 years died.

Thursday, October 23, 1856, Rocky Ridge, Willie Company, Levi Savage Journal. We buried our dead, got up our teams and about nine o'clock a.m. commenced ascending the Rocky Ridge. This was a severe day. The wind blew hard and cold. The ascent was some five miles long and some places steep and covered with deep snow. We became weary, set down to rest, and some became chilled and commenced to freeze. Brothers Atwood, Woodward and myself remained with the teams. They being perfectly loaded down with the sick and children, so thickly stacked I was fearful some would smother. About ten or eleven o'clock in the night we came to a creek [Strawberry Creek] that we did not like to attempt to cross without help, it being full of ice and freezing cold. Leaving Brothers Atwood and Woodard with the teams, I started to the camp for help. I met Brother Willie coming to look for us. He turned for the camp, as he could do no good alone. I passed several on the road and arrived in camp after about four miles of travel. I arrived in camp, but few tents were pitched and men, women, and children sat shivering with cold around their small fires. Some time lapsed when two teams started to bring up the rear. Just before daylight they returned, bringing all with them, some badly frozen, some dying and some dead. It was certainly heart rendering to hear children crying for mothers and mothers crying for children. By the time I got them as comfortably situated as circumstances would admit (which was not very comfortable), day was dawning. I had not shut my eyes for sleep, nor lain down. I was nearly exhausted with fatigue and want of rest.

Thursday, October 23, 1856, Rocky Ridge, Willie Company, History of William James. Sarah James recalls: "The day we [ascended Rocky Ridge][54] I'll never forget as long as I live. It was a bitter cold morning in October as we broke camp. As usual there were dead to be buried before we could go on. Father and Rueben were on the burial detail. Mother, who was helping to pull the heaviest cart, had stayed

---

[54] Sarah James recalled the events described in this entry as taking place on the day they made the Last Crossing of the Sweetwater, but other journals suggest it is probable these events occurred on the day the Willie Company ascended Rocky Ridge.

behind until they could finish their sad work. After a short service we, with my cart ran ahead to catch the rest of the company, and Mother and Rueben started to follow. Father collapsed and fell in the snow. He tried two or three times to get up with Mother's help, then finally he asked her to go on and when he felt rested, he would come on later. Mother knew in her heart that he had given out, but perhaps, she said, in a few minutes with some rest he could come on. She took the cart and hurried to follow us.

"She found us on the riverbank, we were too frightened and tired to cross alone. We had forded this river[55] before many times but it never seemed so far across. It was about 40 feet, I guess, to the other bank. Mother soon had us on our way. The water was icy and soon our clothing was frozen to our bodies. Our feet were frozen numb. Cold and miserable we reached the other bank, put on dry clothing and joined the rest of the company. When we stopped for the night, we made inquiries about our people, but nothing had been heard of them. Since there were some who had been a few hours behind us, we felt they would come with the next group. All night we waited for word. Toward morning some of the Captains who had gone out to gather up the stragglers came into camp bearing the dead body of my Father and the badly frozen body of my brother Rueben. His injuries were so bad that he would suffer from them for the rest of his life. When morning came, Father's body, along with others who had died during the night, were buried in a deep hole. Brush was thrown in and then dirt. A fire was built over the grave to kill the scent to keep the wolves from digging up the remains.

"I can see my Mother's face as she sat looking at the partly conscious group. Her eyes looked so dead that I was

---

[55] Although Sarah James recalled this as crossing the Sweetwater River, it is probable this took place where the trail crossed Strawberry Creek.

157

afraid. She didn't sit long, however, for my Mother was never one to cry. When it was time to move out, Mother had her family ready to go. She put her invalid son in the cart with her baby and we joined the train. Our Mother was a strong woman, and she would see us through anything."

Thursday, October 23, 1856, Rocky Ridge, Willie Company, Jens Pederson Journal. When they were having such hard times with low rations and cold weather, one man decided he didn't want to put up with any more so just said he wasn't going another step. Different ones tried to talk to him and urge him to go on, but had no effect upon his decision. Grandpa, Jens O. Pederson asked for permission to talk to the man. Some told him it wouldn't do any good, so they went on and grandpa tried to reason with him, but that did no good. Finally he said, "Well, if you are not going, I'm going to give you a whipping before I go on," and he slapped him quite hard on the face, and started running to catch up with the company. It made the man angry and he started after grandpa and both of them caught up to the company. The man went on and later thanked grandpa for saving his life.

Thursday, October 23, 1856, Rocky Ridge, Willie Company, John Chislett Journal. A few days of bright freezing weather were succeeded by another snow storm. The day we crossed the Rocky Ridge it was snowing a little --the wind hard from the north-west--and blowing so keenly that it almost pierced us through. We had to wrap ourselves closely in blankets, quilts, or whatever else we could get, to keep from freezing. Captain Willie still attended to the details of the company's travelling, and this day he appointed me to bring up the rear. My duty was to stay behind everything and see that nobody was left along the road. I had to bury a man who had died in my hundred, and I finished doing so after the company had started. In about half an hour, I set out on foot alone to

158

do my duty as rear-guard to the camp. The ascent of the ridge commenced soon after leaving camp, and I had not gone far up it before I overtook a cart that the folks could not pull through the snow, here about knee-deep. I helped them along, and we soon overtook another. By all hands getting to one cart we could travel; so we moved one of the carts a few rods, and then went back and brought up the other. After moving in this way for a while, we overtook other carts at different points of the hill, until we had six carts, not one of which could be moved by the parties owning it. I put our collective strength to three carts at a time, took them a short distance, and the brought up the other three. Thus by travelling over the hill three times--twice forward and once back--I succeeded after hours of toil in bringing my little company to the summit. The six carts were then trotted on gaily down hill, the intense cold stirring us to action. One or two parties who were with these carts gave up entirely, and but for the fact that we overtook one of our ox-teams that had been detained on the road, they must have perished on that Rocky Ridge. One old man, named James[56] (a farm-laborer from Gloucestershire), who had a large family, and who had worked very hard all the way, I found sitting by the roadside unable to pull his cart any farther, I could not get him into the wagon, as it was already overcrowded. He had a shotgun which he had brought from England, and which had been a great blessing to him and his family, for he was a good shot, and often had a mess of sage hens or rabbits for his family. I took the gun from the cart, put a small bundle on the end of it, placed it on his shoulder, and started him out with his little boy, twelve years old. His wife and two daughters older than the boy took the cart along finely after reaching the summit.

We travelled along with the ox-team and overtook

---

[56] Presumably William James.

others, all so laden with the sick and helpless that they moved very slowly. The oxen had almost given out. Some of our folks with carts went ahead of the teams, for where the roads were good they could out-travel oxen; but we constantly overtook some stragglers, some with carts, some without, who had been unable to keep pace with the body of the company. We struggled along in this weary way until after dark, and by this time our "rear" numbered 3 wagons, 8 handcarts, and nearly 40 persons. With the wagons were Mellen Atwood, Levi Savage, and William Woodward, captains of hundreds, faithful men who had worked hard all the way.

We finally came to a stream of water [Strawberry Creek] which was frozen over. We could not see where the company had crossed. If at the point where we struck the creek, then it had frozen over since we passed it. We started one team to cross, but the oxen broke through the ice and would not go over. No amount of shouting and whipping could induce them to stir an inch. We were afraid to try the other teams, for even should they cross we could not leave the one in the creek and go on. There was no wood in the vicinity, so we could make no fire, and were uncertain what to do. We did not know the distance to the camp, but supposed it to be 3 or 4 miles [to Rock Creek]. After consulting about it, we resolved that some one should go on foot to the camp to inform the captain of our situation. I was selected to perform the duty, and I set out with all speed. In crossing the creek I slipped through the ice and got my feet wet, my boots being nearly worn out. I had not gone far when I saw some one sitting by the roadside. I stopped to see who it was, and discovered the old man James and his little boy. The poor old man was quite worn out.

I got him to his feet and had him lean on me, and he walked a little distance, not very far. I partly dragged, partly carried him a short distance farther, but he was quite helpless, and my strength failed me. Being obliged to leave him to go forward on my own errand, I put down a quilt I had wrapped around me, rolled him in it, and told the little boy to walk up and down by his father, and on no account to sit down, or he would be frozen to death. I told him to watch for teams that would come back, and to hail them when they came. This done I again set out for the camp, running nearly all the way and frequently falling down, for there were many obstructions and holes in the road. My boots were frozen stiff, so that I had not the free use of my feet, and it was only by rapid motion that I kept them from being badly frozen. As it was, both were nipped.

After some time I came in sight of the camp fires, which encouraged me. As I neared the camp I frequently overtook stragglers on foot, all pressing forward slowly. I stopped to speak to each one, cautioning them all against resting, as they would surely freeze to death. Finally, about 11 p.m., I reached the camp almost exhausted. I had exerted myself very much during the day in bringing the rear carts up the ridge and had not eaten anything since breakfast. I reported to Captains Willie and Kimball the situation of the folks behind. They immediately got up some horses, and the boys from the Valley started back about midnight to help the ox teams in. The night was very severe and many of the emigrants were frozen. It was 5 a.m. before the last team reached the camp.

I told my companions about the old man James and his little boy. They found the little fellow keeping faithful watch over his father, who lay sleeping in my quilt just as I left him. They lifted him into a wagon, still alive, but in a sort of stupor. He died before morning. His last words were an enquiry as to the safety of his shotgun.

CHAPTER 6
THE TRAIL TO ROCK CREEK

West of the summit of Rocky Ridge, past Strawberry Creek, the trail leads to **Rock Creek**, a stream of water protected by a small hillside covered with rock fragments, and also by many willows and brush near the stream. William Clayton, in his journal entry of June 26, 1847, described it as follows: "At two and three-quarters miles beyond the last small creek, we crossed the branch of the Sweet Water about two rods wide and two feet deep, the water clear and cold. This would be a good camp ground were it not so cold, as it must be from the fact that large deep banks of snow are now lying on its banks both above and below the road. Where the snow doesn't lie, there is good grass and plenty of willow groves for fuel."

At **Rock Creek** the Willie Handcart Company sought refuge from the extreme cold, and buried at least thirteen people. A memorial erected at Rock Creek states: "Captain James G. Willie's Handcart Company of Mormon emigrants on the way to Utah, greatly exhausted by the deep snows of an early winter and suffering from lack of food and clothing, had assembled here for reorganization by relief parties from Utah, about the end of October, 1856. Thirteen persons were frozen to death during a single night and were buried here in one grave. Two others died the next day and were buried nearby. Of the Company of 404 persons, 77 perished before help arrived. The survivors reached Salt Lake City November 9, 1856."

Other pioneers, such as the 1847 Pioneer Company, continued on another couple of miles to the next small stream, called **Willow Creek**. At Willow Creek, William Clayton's entry for June 26, 1847 reads: "Two and a quarter miles beyond [Rock Creek]... we crossed another stream about eight feet wide on an average, though where the ford is, it is nearly three rods wide and two feet deep.   This water is also very clear and the banks well lined with willows and grass.   It is considered a superior camping ground to the one back."

Willie Handcart Company, 1856

Friday, October 24, 1856, Rock Creek, Willie Company, William Woodward, Clerk. Friday, 24 October. Redick N. Allred & others with 6 wagons came to camp this morning to assist the Handcart Company on our journey to the Valley.   It was concluded to stay in camp today & bury the dead as there were 13 persons to inter.   William James, from Pershore, Worcestershire, England, aged 46 died; Elizabeth Bailey, from Leigh, Worcestershire, England, aged 52 died; James Kirkwood from Glasgow, Scotland, aged 11 died; Samuel Gadd, from Orwell, Cambridgeshire, England, aged 10 died; Lars Wendin, from Copenhagen, Denmark, aged 60 died; Anne Olsen, from Seeland, Denmark, aged 46 died; Ella Nilson, from Jutland, Denmark, aged 6 years died; Bodil Mortinsen from Lolland, Denmark, aged 9 years died; Nils Anderson from Seeland, Denmark, aged 41 years died; Ole Madsen from Seeland, Denmark, aged 41 years died.   Many of the Saints have their feet and hands frozen from the severity of the weather.

Friday, October 24, 1856, Rock Creek, Rescue Party and the Willie Company, Journal of Redick Newton Allred. The 24th, I took 6 teams and met them [the Willie Company] 15 miles below in such a hard west wind that they could not travel facing the drifting snow even if they had been ready for duty. I found some dead and dying laying over the camp in the drifting snow that was being piled in heaps by the gale and

163

burying their dead. We set in with the rest to make them as comfortable as possible and remained in camp till next day.

Friday, October 24, 1856, Rock Creek, Willie Company, Levi Savage Journal. This morning found us with thirteen corpses for burial. These were all put into one grave. Some had actually frozen to death. We were obliged to remain in camp, move the tents and people behind the willows to shelter them from the severe wind which blew enough to pierce us through. Several of our cattle died here.

Friday, October 24, 1856, Rock Creek, Willie Company, Joseph B. Elder Journal. The next morning we buried nine all in one deep and wide grave   we rested one day and then again pursued our journey.

Friday, October 24, 1856, Rock Creek, Willie Company, John Chislett Journal. There were so many dead and dying that it was decided to lie by for the day. In the forenoon I was appointed to go round the camp and collect the dead. I took with me two young men to assist me in the sad task, and we collected together, of all ages and both sexes, thirteen corpses, all stiffly frozen. We had a large square hole dug in which we buried these thirteen people, 3 or 4 abreast and 3 deep. When they did not fit in, we put one or two crosswise at the head or feet of the others. We covered them with willows and then with the earth. When we buried these thirteen people some of their relatives refused to attend the services. They manifested an utter indifference about it. The numbness and cold in their physical natures seemed to have reached the soul, and to have crushed out natural feeling and affection. Had I not myself witnessed it, I could not have believed that suffering would have produced such terrible results. But so it was. Two others died during the day, and we buried them in one grave, making fifteen in all buried on that camp ground. It was on Willow Creek [Rock Creek], a tributary of the Sweetwater River. I learned afterwards from men who passed that way the next summer, that the wolves had exhumed the bodies, and their bones were scattered thickly around the vicinity.

Friday, October 24, 1856, Rock Creek, Willie Company, David Reeder Family History.[57] By this time there was very little food left. Winter started early with blinding snow storms. By October 24 they crossed the Wind River Pass and were camped at Rock Creek in the shelter of a hill. During the night of severe cold, 13 of the company perished. The men were weak but all helped to dig a shallow grave, round in shape, and the bodies were placed in it with feet to the center. They were laid away in the clothing they wore. Mary told of her father holding her out to see her playmate lying among the dead as they were placed in the grave. Slender willow boughs were placed over them, then dirt, and finally thin shale was taken from the hill to cover the spot to keep the wolves from disturbing the remains. Two men who helped dig the large grave perished that night and were placed in another grave nearby the side of the other....

Death had occurred frequently during these stages of the journey. On the Sweetwater, these immigrants encountered extreme winter weather and heavy snows. During one of these severe storms, 13 died in one night and were buried in one grave. After the bodies were placed in the grave their heads around the outside with their feet to the center, James lifted his small daughter Mary up so she could see them. At the age of 88 she could still visualize the scene. At Rock Creek within 300 miles of Salt Lake they had two very sick children and no provisions of any kind. James went to gather some sage brush

---

[57] Compiled by Adolph Madsen Reeder.

to make a fire and while doing so, he found some pieces of raw hide. He gathered them up took them to camp. They cleaned, scraped and cooked them and gave them to the little ones who ate them with a relish.

Friday, October 24, 1856, Rock Creek, Willie Company, Jens Neilson History. After consuming their last pound of flour days before, it was here that Jens and Elsie gained a victory over almost certain death through their great physical strength, indomitable courage and unconquerable spirits. Their strength had carried them beyond the endurance of the other four men in their camp who had succumbed to the snow, cold, starvation and exhaustion, and had been buried in shallow graves under the snow [at Rock Creek]. Also buried was Jens' and Elsie's six-year old son, Neils and the Mortensen girl [Bodil Mortensen]. The end appeared to be near and certain for Jens. His feet became so frozen he could not walk another step, which caused his right foot to be at right angles the rest of his life. At this point Jens said to Elsie, "Leave me by the trail in the snow to die, and you go ahead and try to keep up with the company and save your life." If you believe men have a monopoly on strength and courage, then pay heed to Elsie's immortal words when she said, "Ride, I can't leave you, I can pull the cart." Jens had to suffer the humiliation of riding while Elsie pulled like an ox. He later said when describing this ordeal, "No person can describe it, nor could it be comprehended or understood by any human living in this life, but those who were called to pass through it."

October 1856, Rock Creek and vicinity, Willie Company, George Cunningham Journal. The weather turned to be extremely cold and many died from the effect of want and cold. I myself have helped to bury (or partly bury, as they were only put a small distance underground--might just

166

as well have been left open for the wolves) 10-15 in a single day. Our Captain intended to keep his word, and commenced to kill off the cattle but they were nearly as poor as we were. We used to boil the bones and drink the soup and eat what little meat there was. We greedily devoured the hides also. I myself had took a piece of hide when I could get it, scorched off hair, roasted it a little on the coals, cut it into little pieces so that I could swallow it and bolted it down my throat for supper and thought it was most delicious. Many were frozen to death. I think that there were only five or six men in camp towards the last but what were badly frozen. Our Captain drove all he could and did his duty. He was frozen and came very close to dying. Some would sacrifice themselves by giving their food or perhaps some old blanket that covered them. In common cares, we cannot tell what our friends and neighbors are, but there are circumstances which undoubtedly proved them.

While laboring under those trials and afflictions I lay down one night and fell asleep. I dreamed a dream, that morning had come, the storm had subsided some and that we had started out on the road. I thought that I saw two men coming toward us on horseback. They were riding very swiftly and soon came up to us. They said that they had volunteered to come to our rescue and that they would go on further east to meet a company which was still behind us and that on the morrow, we could meet a number of wagons loaded with provisions for us. They were dressed in blue soldier overcoats and had Spanish saddles on their horses. I examined them, particularly the saddles, as they were new to me. I also could discern every expression of their countenance. They seemed to rejoice and be exceedingly glad that they had come to our relief and saved us. At last morning came, it had cleared somewhat and I think that the snow was 18 inches deep on the level where we were. The weather was very cold. We made some very large fires with willows which were abundant around the place, and everyone stood around the fires with gloomy faces. The thought of my dream would be fulfilled for it was my promise in my blessing to dream dreams and see things come to pass. We therefore set out and to our great pleasure, everything in my dream was fulfilled. I can recall that I was on the lead of the group being somewhat inspired by which I had dreamed the previous night. The day was rather blustery with alternate snowstorms blowing from the north mixed with clear spells which lasted sometimes for nearly half an hour. During one of the clear spells I spotted two persons that I had dreamed of the night before, riding fast towards us. I called the fact to the attention of the crowd, being quite a distance off. I roared out, "Here they come, see them coming over that hill." They told me I was a true dreamer, and we all felt that we should thank God. I met the wagons with the provisions on the following day. We were very well treated by the brethren who came to meet us. Now the great difficulty was in eating too much. The feeling and senses of our people were dull and numbed now. Everyone feared death, and seemed indifferent and stupefied.

One overrider said, "Oh death where is thy sting? Oh, grave, where is thy victory?" It had gone too far to dread death, for the threat of life had by this time been nearly exhausted. Neither had the grave much victory to boast of for many did not feel like going one step out of its way. Our Captain showed us all a noble example. He was furnished a mule to ride on our start from Iowa City, but he said, "I will never get on its back, I will show the example, you follow it." He did so and the Captains of hundreds followed him. They would crowd on ahead to be the first into the streams to help the women and children across. After getting the last one across they would crowd on ahead to be the first. They were completely exhausted and had to be hauled the balance of the way. Some of them not being able to stand on their feet. Their names were: James Willy, Mellen Attwood, Levi Savage,

William Woodward, and the fifth was a Danish brother whose name I can't recall.

Martin Handcart Company, 1856

Monday, November 17, 1856, Rock Creek, Martin Company, John Jaques Journal. At the Aspen Grove camp,[58] I have been told, sixteen corpses were interred. Several discoveries were made on the journey. The way to have a warm sleeping place was this--sweep away the ashes of the camp fire and lay your bed on the spot where the fire had been built. You would be sure to sleep warm there, if anywhere. In the morning the same spot was found to be the most available for a graver use--it was the easiest place in which to dig a grave to bury the night's dead. Thus, in this severe winter traveling and camping economy, the earth served three separate, distinct and important purposes.

---

[58] This location is probably in error--the reference should be to Rock Creek.

CHAPTER 7
COMPLETING THE JOURNEY

From Rock Creek, the Mormon Trail continues west, through hundreds of miles and many additional challenges. Only a few of those are mentioned here. The pioneers reached the **Last Crossing of the Sweetwater** at what is now called the **Burnt Ranch**. From there, the trail climbs to **South Pass**, an important point because it marks the **Continental Divide**, where water to the east drains to the Atlantic Ocean and water to the west drains to the Pacific Ocean. Not surprisingly, the first springs west of South Pass were called **Pacific Springs**. William Clayton's Emigrant Guide specifically mentions South Pass: "South Pass, or summit of dividing ridge. This is the dividing ridge between the waters of the Atlantic and Pacific. Altitude, 7,085 feet."

A publication of the U.S. Department of the Interior summarizes the trail as follows: "All emigrants on the Oregon Trail in Wyoming followed the North Platte River, the Sweetwater River, and reached or crossed South Pass before making a choice of several routes of travel to places further west. At South Pass, one of the most significant historic sites in the state of Wyoming, emigrants negotiated a major range of the Rocky Mountains, crossing the Continental Divide that separates the Atlantic from the Pacific watershed. At the dividing line, also, they left American territory and entered Oregon Country. About nine miles east of South Pass was a convenient camping area along a grassy stream bottom. Here the trail crossed the Sweetwater River for the ninth and last time since striking it about one hundred miles east, near Independence Rock. The camping place at this Ninth or Last Crossing was an approximate halfway point for those traveling from the Missouri River to Oregon's Willamette Valley."

Few places in western North America are as historically significant as **South Pass** and the area surrounding it. Testimony to that significance can be found in unnumbered diaries of emigrant travelers. As one person has written, "It is nearly impossible to find a contemporary diary (of Oregon Trail travelers) from 1836 to 1866 that does not mention South Pass." When we stand on South Pass today, it is difficult to visualize the full sweep of history that makes it so important in the history of the United States. It was central to the embodiment of the American dream of expansion across the North American Continent to the frontiers beyond the Rocky Mountains. South Pass is one of those historic sites which should be preserved for future generations, or so long as the Republic should endure. Our United States would probably not exist in its present form if the gentle, broad pass known as South Pass had not existed. It is difficult to grasp that truth today; we are too far removed from those momentous days when our country was young and in its most formative stages. "It was the gate through which the United States would reach its empire...." South Pass remains today as one of the unrecognized shrines of Manifest Destiny. South Pass and the Great Divide Basin are geologic mysteries. Why the great granite up-thrusts of the main Rocky Mountain chain should be interrupted between the Wind River Mountains of Wyoming and the Colorado Rockies to the south cannot be explained. What is located there between them is a high, dry desert in south-central Wyoming. The Continental Divide drops from elevations of 13,000 and more feet in the Wind Rivers to elevations averaging around 7,000 to 7,500 feet across South Pass and the Great Divide Basin. South Pass lies between the Wind River Mountains to the north and the Oregon Buttes to the south. The actual crossing of the Continental Divide by the Oregon Trail in South Pass is through a swale at an elevation of 7,412 feet. The Divide proceeds on south to Oregon Buttes and there splits to completely encircle the Great Divide Basin.

171

Eventually, of course, all the pioneer companies reached the Salt Lake Valley. Many of the events associated with completing the journey are inspiring, and a few are included here as a small sample of the relief and joy felt by those faithful saints who endured the hardships and made the sacrifices required of them.

1847 Pioneer Company

Sunday, June 27, 1847, South Pass, Pioneer Company, William Clayton. Sunday, 27th. Morning fine but cold. The ox teams started at five minutes to eight and the remainder shortly after. We soon met eight of the Oregon men on their way back, having over twenty horses and mules with them mostly laden with packs of robes, skins, etc. Several of the brethren sent letters back by them. At two and three-quarters miles, arrived at the dividing ridge where Elder Pratt took a barometrical observation and found the altitude 7,085 feet above the level of the sea. This spot is 278-1/2 miles from Fort John and is supposed to divide the Oregon and Indian Territory by a line running north and south. At two miles farther we arrived at where Elder Pratt camped last night on the head waters of the Green River and although the stream is small, we have the satisfaction of seeing the current run west instead of east. The face of the country west looks level except far in the distance where a range of mountains peers up, their surface white with snow. There is good grass here but no timber nor in fact any in sight except on the mountains....

It is 3 years today since our brethren Joseph and Hyrum were taken from us and it was a general feeling to spend the day in fasting and prayer, but the gentile companies being close in our rear and feed scarce it was considered necessary to keep ahead for the benefit of our teams, but many minds have reverted back to the scenes at Carthage Jail, and it is a gratification that we have so far prospered in our endeavors to get from under the grasp of our enemies.

Monday, June 28, 1847, Dry Sandy Creek, Wyoming, 1847 Pioneer Company. The Pioneers encountered Jim Bridger, headed east toward Fort Laramie with two companions. By one account, he was so "likered up" he could hardly sit on his horse.[59] Brigham Young and the other leaders were anxious for any information they could obtain. Erastus Snow's Journal recorded: "Mr. Bridger ... camped with us and gave us much information relative to roads, streams, and country generally." Brigham Young's Manuscript History includes the famous interchange: "Bridger considered it imprudent to bring a large population into the Great Basin until it was ascertained that grain could be raised; he said he would give $1,000 for a bushel of corn raised in that basin." President Young replied: "Wait a little, and we will show you."

Wednesday, July 21, 1847, "Last Creek Canyon" (today's Emigration Canyon), 1847 Pioneer Company, Orson Pratt. [Orson Pratt's advance company was slightly ahead of Brigham Young due to President Young's illness. Orson Pratt and his company climbed a steep hill near the valley to get a clear view.] From the top ... a broad open valley, about 20 miles wide and 30 long, lay stretched out before us, at the north end of which the broad waters of the Great Salt Lake glistened in the sunbeams, containing high mountainous islands from 25 to 30 miles in extent. After issuing from the mountains among which we had been shut up for many days, and beholding in a moment such an extensive scenery open before us, we could not refrain from a shout of

---

[59] See Kimball, Stanley B., Heber C. Kimball, Mormon Patriarch and Pioneer, p. 166.

joy which almost involuntarily escaped from our lips the moment this grand and lovely scenery was within our view.

Friday, July 23, 1847, Big Mountain (east of Salt Lake City), Rear Company of the 1847 Pioneer Company, Brigham Young. I ascended and crossed over the Big Mountain, when on its summit I directed Elder Woodruff, who had kindly tendered me the use of his carriage, to turn the same half way round so that I could have a view of a portion of Salt Lake Valley. The spirit of light rested upon me and hovered over the valley, and I felt that there the Saints would find protection and safety. We descended and encamped at the foot of the Little Mountain.

Friday, July 23, 1847, Big Mountain (east of Salt Lake City), Rear Company of the 1847 Pioneer Company, Howard Egan Journal. My heart felt truly glad, and I rejoiced at having the privilege of beholding this extensive and beautiful valley, that may yet become a home for the Saints. From this point we could see the blue waters of the Salt Lake. By ascending one of the ridges at the mouth of this canyon, the view over the valley is at once pleasing and interesting. These high mountains on the east side, extending to the head of the valley about fifty miles to the south, many of them white on the tops and crevices with snow. At the south end is another mountain, which bounds the valley in that direction, and at its western extremity it is joined by another range, forming its western boundary to the valley and extending in a northerly direction until it ceases abruptly nearly west of this place. The valley between these mountains is judged to be twenty-five to thirty miles wide at the north end of the last mentioned mountain. The level valley extends to the Salt Lake which is plainly visible for many miles in a western direction from this place. In the lake, and many miles beyond this valley are two mountains projecting high in the air, forming a solemn but pleasing contrast with the dark blue waters of the lake. Beyond these two mountains and in the distance, in a direction between them, is another high dark mountain supposed to be on the western boundary of the lake, and judged to be eighty to one hundred miles from here. At this distance we can see, apparently, but a small surface of the water, extending between this valley and the mountains referred to, but that surface is probably thirty miles wide. Looking to the northwest, another mountain appears, extending to the north till hidden by the eastern range. At the base of this mountain is a long ridge of white substance, which from its bright shining appearance is doubtless salt, and was probably caused by the dashing of the waves and then hardened by the sun. . . .

This valley is bounded by high mountains, some of them covered with snow and from what knowledge we have of it at present, this is the most safe and secure place the Saints could possibly locate themselves in. Nature has fortified this place on all sides, with only a few narrow passes, which could be made impregnable without much difficulty. The scarcity of timber has probably been the reason that this beautiful valley has not been settled long since by the Gentiles. But I think we can find sufficient timber up the creeks for present purposes, and also coal in the mountains. The saints have reason to rejoice, and thank the Lord for this goodly land unpopulated by the Gentiles.

Saturday, July 24, 1847, Great Salt Lake, Pioneer Company, William Clayton. Saturday, 24th. The plowing is renewed and many are gone to planting potatoes. There is one drag going. Others are still at work on the dams. John Pack and Joseph Mathews returned at dark last night and reported the President and company a few miles up Last Creek. They have gone back this morning to fix two bridges at the mouth of the canyon. The day is fine and hot with a nice breeze. At a quarter to twelve, President Young and Kimball arrived and the

175

wagons also began to arrive at the same time. The President seems much better and the sick generally are getting better. Most of the brethren express themselves well pleased with the place, but some complain because there is no timber.... About 5:00 p.m. we were favored with another nice shower accompanied by thunder and some wind. It continued raining till nearly dark; the balance of the evening fine. Elder Kimball says that it is contemplated to send out an exploring party to start on Monday and proceed north to the Bear River and Cache valleys. They design taking several wagons with them and Presidents Young and Kimball accompany the expedition. Another company is to start at the same time and go west to the lake, then south to the Utah Lake and return down this valley.

Saturday, July 24, 1847, Great Salt Lake, Pioneer Company, Wilford Woodruff Journal. July 24th This is an important day in the History of my life and the History of the Church of JESUS CHRIST of Latter Day Saints. On this important day after trav[eling] from our encampment 6 miles through the deep ravine, valley, ending with the canyon through the last creek we came in full view of the great valley or Basin [of] the Salt Lake and land of promise held in reserve by the hand of GOD for a resting place for the Saints upon which a portion of the Zion of GOD will be built.

We gazed with wonder and admiration upon the vast rich fertile valley which lay for about 25 miles in length & 16 miles in width clothed with the heaviest garb of green vegetation in the midst of which lay a large lake of Salt water of [ ] miles in extent in which could be seen large Islands & mountains towering towards the clouds also the glorious valley abounding with the best fresh water springs rivulets creeks & brooks & rivers of various sizes all of which gave animation to the sporting trout & other fish while the waters were wending their way into the great Salt lake. Our hearts were surely made glad after a hard journey from Winter Quarters of 1,200 miles through flats of Platt Rivers steeps of the Black Hills & the Rocky mountains and burning sands of the eternal Sage regions & willow swales & Rocky Canyons & stubs & stones, to gaze upon a valley of such vast extent entirely surrounded with a perfect chain of everlasting hills & mountains covered with eternal snow with their innumerable peaks like Pyramids towering towards Heaven presenting probably that could be obtained on the globe.

Thoughts of pleasing meditations ran in rapid succession through our minds while we contemplated that not many years that the House of GOD would stand upon the top of the Mountains while the valleys would be converted into orchard, vineyard, gardens & fields by the inhabitants of Zion & the standard be unfurled for the nations to gather there to.

President Young expressed his full satisfaction in the appearance of the valley as a resting place for the Saints & was amply repaid for his Journey.... Our Brethren who had arrived 2 days before had pitched their encampment upon the bank of two small streams of pure water & had commenced plowing. Had broke about 5 acres of ground & commenced planting potatoes.

As soon as we were formed in the encampment before I took my dinner having 1/2 a bushel of potatoes I repaired to the plowed field & planted my potatoes hoping with the blessings of God at least to save the Seed for another year.

Saturday, July 24, 1847, Great Salt Lake, Pioneer Company, Wilford Woodruff, Sermon delivered in Salt Lake City on July 24, 1880. On the twenty-fourth I drove my carriage, with President Young lying on a bed in it, into the open valley, the rest of the company following. When we came out of the canyon, into full view of the valley, I turned the side of my carriage around, open to the west, and President Young arose from his bed and took a survey of the country. While gazing on the scene before us, he was enwrapped in vision for several minutes. He had seen the valley before in vision, and upon the occasion he saw the future glory of Zion and Israel, as they would be, planted in the valleys of the mountains. When the vision had passed, he said, "It is enough. This is the right place. Drive on." So I drove to the encampment already formed by those who had come along in advance of us.

Willie Handcart Company, 1856

Saturday, October 25, 1856, Last Crossing of the Sweetwater/ Burnt Ranch, Willie Company, William Woodward, Clerk. Rolled from camp in the morning. Thomas Gurdlestone from Great Melton, Norwich, aged 62 years died. William Groves, from Cranmoor, Somersetshire, England, aged 22 years died. Crossed the Sweetwater for the last time. Travelled about 15 miles & camped on the Sweetwater. Some brethren were stationed at this post on the river with supplies of flour & onions. John Walters from Bristol, Somerset, England, aged ___ died. William Smith from Eldersfield, Worcestershire, England, aged 48 years died.

Saturday, October 25, 1856, Last Crossing of the Sweetwater/ Burnt Ranch, Willie Company, Levi Savage Journal (last entry in this journal). We commenced our march again. From this I have not been able to keep a daily journal, but nothing of much note transpired, except the people died daily. Theophilus Cox died on the morning of the 7th of November, on the Webber, was carried to Cottonwood Grove, East Canyon Creek, and there buried. We overtook Brother Smoot's company in emigration on the 9th. That afternoon we arrived in Great Salt Lake City and deposited the people among the Saints, where they were made comfortable.

Sunday, November 9, 1856, Salt Lake City, Willie

Company, William Woodward, Clerk. Early this morning, the people were busy preparing to enter the Valley. Rhoda R. Oakey from Eldersfield, Worcestershire, England, aged 11 years died this morning. The teams after some difficulty ascended the Little mountain and rolled down Emigration Canyon. Several of the wagons passed Captain Smoot's Church train in the canyon. The wagons formed in order on the bench at the mouth of the canyon & rolled into the city. Captain Smoot's train went ahead. F. D. Richards, S. W. Richards & many others came to meet us on the Bench and went ahead of us into the City. As soon as the company arrived in the City of Great Salt Lake, the Bishops of the different wards took every person that was not provided for a home & put them into comfortable quarters. Hundreds of persons were round the wagons on our way thro' the city welcoming the company safely home.

Sunday, November 9, 1856, Salt Lake City, Willie Company, Church Chronology--Andrew Jenson. Capt. James G. Willie's handcart company arrived in G.S.L. City, after great sufferings from scarcity of provisions, cold and over-exertion in the mountains. It left Iowa City, Iowa,... with 120 handcarts and six wagons, numbering about five hundred souls, of whom 66 died on the journey. Captain Abraham O. Smoot's wagon train arrived the same day.

Sunday, November 9, 1856, Salt Lake City, Willie Company, Hosea Stout Journal. Smoot's Company and the Company of Hand Carts Came in the afternoon. There was some 100 wagons. They seemed to be in good heart.

November 1856, Salt Lake City, Willie Company, George Cunningham Journal. At last we arrived in Salt Lake where we were kindly cared for and well treated. The sick were doctored and then sent to the area settlements. We were sent to American Fork where my home has been ever since. Here we met with many old acquaintances and soon found new ones.

Martin Handcart Company, 1856

Tuesday, November 18, 1856, Last Crossing of the Sweetwater/ Burnt Ranch, Martin Company with Rescue Party, Journal of Redick Newton Allred. Captain Grant got into my camp on the 17th of November [more likely the 18th, based upon R.T. Burton's account and John Jaques Journal] just 30 days since he left me and saluted me with "Hurrah for the bulldog, good for hanging on."

The teams having all arrived we were again organized into companies of tens by wagons each 10 taking up a company of 100 as they were organized in their handcarts--my 10 wagons hauling Captain Mayo's Company[60]. All could ride altho much crowded. We then set out for the city with this half starved, half frozen and almost entirely exhausted company of about 500 Saints. But from that time on they did not suffer with hunger or fatigue but all suffered more or less with cold. As well as I was provided I even lost my toenails from frost.

Wednesday, November 19, 1856, Little Sandy, Wyoming, Martin Company, John Jaques Journal. On the 19th the company camped at Little Sandy, having sagebrush for fuel, and on the 20th on the Big Sandy. Cold enough it was at all the camping places but that was a most searchingly cold night on the latter river. It seemed impossible to get warm sleeping in a wagon. It was warmer sleeping with beds on the ground, where, if the biting, frosty air got the upper hand of you, it could not get the underside of you as well, but it could

---

[60] This is a reference to Peter Mayo, from Lancashire, England.

do both in a wagon.

Wednesday, November 19, 1856, Little Sandy, Wyoming, Martin Company, Patience Loader Recollection. A good brother, who owned a wagon told us we could sleep in it. He would make a hole in the snow and make his bed there. He thought we would be warmer sleeping in the wagon. We made our bed there but we only had one old quilt to lie on and in the night I woke up and called to mother. "I am freezing." The side I had been laying on was so benumbed with cold that mother got up and helped me out of the wagon. There were some big fires burning in several places in the camp and lots of the sisters were sitting and sleeping near the fire to keep warm. So I went to a fire and stayed there the remainder of the night. In the morning we traveled on again as usual. One great blessing we had more food to eat. We got our pound of flour a day and sometimes a little meat and very soon we were all able to ride instead of walking, and we could stay in the wagons at nights. After we baked our bread, we put the hot coals in our bake oven and took it in the wagon and that made it quite comfortable and warm for us to sleep. I can remember how kind the brethren were to us poor, distressed miserable looking creatures. I think we must have looked a very deplorable set of human beings to them when they first met us. What brave men they must have been to start out from Salt Lake City in the middle of winter in search of us poor folks.

November 1856, Fort Bridger, Martin Company, Ephraim Hanks Recollections. One evening after having gone as far as Ft. Bridger, I was requested by a sister to come and administer to her son, whose name was Thomas Dobson. He was very sick indeed and his friends expected he would die that night. When I came to the place where he lay he was moaning pitifully, and was almost too weak to turn around in his bed. I felt the power of God resting upon me and

181

addressing the young man said, "Will you believe the words I tell you?" His response was, "Yes." I then administered to him and he was immediately healed. He got up, dressed himself and danced the hornpipe on the inboard of a wagon, which I procured for that purpose. But notwithstanding these manifestations of the Lord's goodness, many of the emigrants whose extremities were frozen, lost their limbs, either in whole or part. Many such I washed with water and castile soap, until the frozen parts would fall off, after which I would sever the shreds of flesh from the remaining portion of the limbs with my scissors. Some of the emigrants lost toes, other things and again others whole hands and feet; one woman who now resides in Koosharem, Piute Co., Utah, lost both her legs below the knees, and quite a number who survived became cripples for life. But so far as I remember there were no fresh cases of frozen limbs after my arrival in camp. As the train moved forward in the day time I would generally leave the road in search of game; and on these expeditions killed and dressed a number of buffaloes, distributing their meat among the people. On one occasion when I was lagging behind with a killed buffalo, an English girl by the name of Griffin gave out completely, and not being able to walk any further, she lay down with her head in the snow. When I saw her disabled condition I lifted her on my saddle the horse being loaded with buffalo meat, and in this condition she rode into camp.

Soon more relief companies were met and as fast as the baggage was transferred into the wagons, the hand carts were abandoned one after another, until none were left.

I remained with the immigrants until the last of Captain Martin's company arrived in Salt Lake City on the thirtieth day of November, 1856.

Wednesday, November 26, 1856, near Echo Canyon, Martin Company, John Jaques Journal. The next camp was in a small canyon running out of the north side of Echo

Canyon, a few miles above the mouth of the latter. Here a birth took place, and one of the relief party generously contributed part of his under linen to clothe the little stranger. The mother did quite as well as could have been expected, considering the unpropitious circumstances. So did the father who subsequently became a prosperous merchant of this city. The little newcomer also did well, and was named Echo Squires.

Saturday, November 29, 1856, Emigration Canyon, Utah, Martin Company and Rescue Companies, R.T. Burton Account. Passed over Big Mountain, snowing fast. Stopped snowing after noon. Passed over Little Mountain; camped in the head of Emigration Canyon; met supplies.

Saturday, November 29, 1856, Emigration Canyon, Utah, Martin Company and Rescue Companies, Harvey Cluff Journal. Reaching East Creek at the base of the Big Mountain, the snow was about four feet deep, a recent fall of snow having filled up the track. Now came the tug of war so to speak. Every available man lined up in double file as far apart as the wagon wheels and thus they proceeded up the mountain in advance of the train. At regular distances we would make a side track for the lead teams to pull out and fall in behind, thus we continued up and up the four miles and near the summit a cut with shovels had to be made through a snow drift twenty feet deep. The whole day was consumed in getting over the mountain and camp was made between the Big and Little Mountains.

Saturday, November 29, 1856, Salt Lake City, reference to Martin Company, Wilford Woodruff Journal. President [Jedediah M.] Grant had a vary sick night the worst that He has [had] since he had been sick. The Devil worked hard all night to kill his body. The brethren laid hands upon him many times & rebuked the devil.... It was a perfect warfare all night. He is easier this morning.

We get word this morning from the Hand Cart company that they will Camp to night at Killion's at the foot of the Little Mountain. Many of them are frozen. Their fingers & toes are dropping off & flesh dropping off their bones. It has been vary bad management in starting out companies so late upon the plains. Brother Decker Came in last night. He brought in the express. He says the ox trains [Hunt and Hodgett] Cannot even get to Bridger.... There has never been so much suffering among any people as their is this season. It is truly deplorable.

Sunday, November 30, 1856, Salt Lake City, Martin Company and Rescue Parties, R.T. Burton Account. This morning started early; arrived in S.L. City a little before noon with all the hand cart company and several families from the ox-trains. Had in the trains 351 horses and mules, 104 wagons and 32 oxen.

Sunday, November 30, 1856, Salt Lake City, Martin Company and Rescue Parties, William Broomhead Diary. Came into the city about 1/2 past eleven on Sunday the [30th] day of November. The day was fine. I was greeted home by my wife and friends with joy. Went to meeting that night and heard some good instructions.

Sunday, November 30, 1856, Salt Lake City, Martin Company and Rescue Parties, Wilford Woodruff Journal. I attended meeting at the Tabernacle... some remarks [were] made By President Young concerning the Hand Cart Company who was now entering the City.... We went into the street & saw the poor saints who had just arrived. Their was about 100 wagons containing the Company. Many were Cripples. Had their hands & feet froze nearly off. They were immediately distributed through the City.

Sunday, November 30, 1856, Salt Lake City, Martin Company and Rescue Parties, Journal of Redick Newton Allred. We arrived in the city in triumph. Captain Burton leading one and I the other as we moved up the street in two lines to the tithing yard where we were greeted with much praise and a hardy welcome to the city of the saints where we as well as the new comers could rest from our labors and our work could follow us.

Thus ended one of the hardest and most successful missions I have ever performed, for although the mission with the Mormon Battalion was long, hard, tedious and therefore very severe, yet this was short and sharp in the extreme. President Kimball blessed me from the stand with a multiplicity of blessings for my integrity and labors in not leaving my post but sticking by to the last under trying circumstances and influences.

Sunday, November 30, 1856, Salt Lake City, Martin Company and Rescue Parties, Journal of Langley Allgood Bailey.[61] We arrived in Salt Lake City Sunday noon. Coming

---

[61] Langley Allgood Bailey was born March 27, 1838 in Whitwick England. He was 18 years old when he journeyed with the Martin company. On the way he became very ill and was told by a doctor that he "must not go another step or [he] would die and be buried on the roadside." F. D. Richards and C. H. Wheelock administered to him and promised him that he would live to reach the valley.

One morning he started out ahead of the company, in his words, "…to get away, lay down under a sagebrush and die. I saw my father and mother and my cart pass by, I stretched out to die; just then a voice said 'your mother is hunting you jump up.' I saw mother in haste coming towards me wanting to know what had gone wrong with me. I told her I had planned to lay down and die. I felt it was too much to pull me on the cart, at the same time have as much luggage they could manage, [she] scolded me a little. She

185

out of Emigration canyon I was lifted up in the wagon [and] could see houses in the distance. It was like the Israelites of old and beholding the promised land.

Wednesday, December 10, 1856, Salt Lake City, Historian's Journal. Ferramozas Little and Ephraim Hanks started in the afternoon with the mail east.

Thursday, December 11, 1856, Salt Lake City, Arrival of Some of Hunt and Hodgett Wagon Companies, Mary Goble Pay.[62] My mother never got well.... She died between the Little and Big Mountains.... She was forty three years of age. We arrived in Salt Lake City nine o'clock at night the eleventh of December, 1856. Three out of the four that were living were frozen. My mother was dead in the wagon....

Early next morning Brigham Young came.... When he saw our condition, our feet frozen and our mother dead, tears rolled down his cheeks....

The doctor amputated my toes... while the sisters were dressing mother for her grave.... That afternoon she was buried.

I have often thought of my mother's words before we left England. "Polly, I want to go to Zion while my children are small so that they can be raised in the Gospel of Jesus Christ."

---

reminded [me] what I was promised by apostle Franklin D. Richards. I rode on a cart until the teams from the valley met us."

[62] As quoted by President Gordon B. Hinckley, Ensign, July 1984, p.6.

Monday, December 15, 1856, Salt Lake City, Last Arrival of Hunt and Hodgett Companies, Wilford Woodruff Journal. It is a fair day. The remainder of the Emigration all arrived in the City to day about 30 teams containing about 200 souls it being the Last of the ox train Company.

Years Later, Cedar City, Martin Company, Francis Webster.[63] Years later, a group in Cedar City were talking about [those] who were in those ill-fated companies. Members of the group spoke critically of the Church and its leaders because the company of converts had been permitted to start so late in the season. [A manuscript in the possession of President Hinckley states:]

"One old man in the corner sat silent and listened as long as he could stand it. Then he arose and said things that no person who heard will ever forget. His face was white with emotion, yet he spoke calmly, deliberately, but with great earnestness and sincerity.

"He said in substance, 'I ask you to stop this criticism. You are discussing a matter you know nothing about. Cold historic facts mean nothing here for they give no proper interpretation of the questions involved. A mistake to send the handcart company out so late in the season? Yes. But I was in that company and my wife was in it and Sister Nellie Unthank whom you have cited was there too. We suffered beyond anything you can imagine and many died of exposure and starvation, but did you ever hear a survivor of that

---

[63] At age 26, Francis Webster had been a member of the Martin Company along with his wife and infant child. He became a leader in the Church and a leader in the communities of Southern Utah. The majority of this entry is as quoted by President Gordon B. Hinckley, Ensign, November 1991, p. 54, with the last paragraph of the entry as quoted by President James E. Faust, Ensign, May 1979, p. 53.

company utter a word of criticism? Not one of that company ever apostatized or left the Church because every one of us came through with the absolute knowledge that God lives, for we became acquainted with him in our extremities.'

"'I have pulled my handcart when I was so weak and weary from illness and lack of food that I could hardly put one foot ahead of the other. I have gone on [to some point I thought I could never reach, only to feel that] the cart began pushing me. I have looked back many times to see who was pushing my cart, but my eyes saw no one. I knew then that the angels of God were there.'"

October 6, 1991, General Conference, Salt Lake City, President Gordon B. Hinckley.[64] I wish to remind everyone within my hearing that the comforts we have, the peace we have, and, most important, the faith and knowledge of the things of God that we have, were bought with a terrible price by those who have gone before us. Sacrifice has always been a part of the gospel of Jesus Christ. The crowning element of our faith is our conviction of our living God, the Father of us all, and of His Beloved Son, the Redeemer of the world. It is because of our Redeemer's life and sacrifice that we are here. It is because of His sacrificial atonement that we and all of the sons and daughters of God will partake of the salvation of the Lord....

In our own helplessness, He becomes our rescuer, saving us from damnation and bringing us to eternal life. In times of despair, in seasons of loneliness and fear, He is there on the horizon to bring succor and comfort and assurance and faith. He is our King, our Savior, our Deliverer, our Lord and our God.

Those on the high, cold plains of Wyoming came to

---

[64] Ensign, November 1991, pp. 54-55.

know Him in their extremity as perhaps few come to know Him. But to every troubled soul, every man or woman in need, to those everywhere who are pulling heavy burdens through the bitter storms of life, He has said: "Come unto me, all ye that labor and are heavy laden, and I will give you rest. Take my yoke upon you, and learn of me; for I am meek and lowly in heart; and ye shall find rest unto your souls. For my yoke is easy and my burden is light." (Matt. 11:28-30.)

Now, I am grateful that today none of our people are stranded on the Wyoming highlands. But I know that all about us there are many who are in need of help and who are deserving of rescue. Our mission in life, as followers of the Lord Jesus Christ, must be a mission of saving. There are the homeless, the hungry, the destitute. Their condition is obvious. We have done much. We can do more to help those who live on the edge of survival.... It is not those on the high plains of Wyoming that we need be concerned with today. It is with many immediately around us, in our families, in our wards and stakes, in our neighborhoods and communities. "And the Lord called his people Zion, because they were of one heart and one mind, and dwelt in righteousness; and there was no poor among them." (Moses 7:18.) If we are to build that Zion of which the prophets have spoken and of which the Lord has given mighty promise, we must set aside our consuming selfishness. We must rise above our love for comfort and ease, and in the very process of effort and struggle, even in our extremity, we shall become better acquainted with our God.

Let us never forget that we have a marvelous heritage received from great and courageous people who endured unimaginable suffering and demonstrated unbelievable courage for the cause they loved. You and I know what we should do. God help us to do it when it needs to be done, I humbly pray in the name of Jesus Christ, amen.

ACKNOWLEDGEMENTS

The majority of journal entries included in this book were obtained from and are used courtesy of The Church of Jesus Christ of Latter-day Saints, Historical Department Archives, and the Utah State Historical Society. Certain specific entries are also used by permission or courtesy of descendants of those quoted. The editors wish to express gratitude for access to these materials.

For additional copies, please contact:

Stewart Glazier
(801) 572-5924
2129 E. Willow Brook Way
Sandy, UT 84092

or

Devin Glazier
(801) 368-1572